The Garden of Eating

The Garden of Eating

---•---—---•---—---•---—---•---

Food, Sex, and
the Hunger for Meaning

JEREMY IGGERS

BasicBooks
A Division of HarperCollins*Publishers*

FIRST EDITION

Designed by Laura Lindgren

ISBN 0-465-07805-2

96 97 98 99 00 ❖/RRD 10 9 8 7 6 5 4 3 2 1

To my parents

Contents

Acknowledgments

I want to express my appreciation to everyone who helped me with this project. To Lynette Lamb and Jay Walljasper for proposing my original *Utne Reader* magazine essay on food and guilt, and to Steve Fraser for inviting me to expand my ideas into a book. And to my editor at Basic Books, Gail Winston, for offering just the right mix of prodding, encouragement, and helpful suggestions.

I also want to thank all the friends and colleagues who offered support, suggestions, and constructive criticism: Toni Allegra, Tom Atchison, Julie Caniglia, Ross Carson, Anne de Meurisse, Lisa Disch, Kathleen Fluegel, Jim Glassman, Susan Heineman, Lisa Heldke, Karen Hess, Dan Iggers, Rhona Leibel, Elaine May, Lary May, Kathy Papatola, Riv-Ellen Prell, Susan Reed, Ron Salzberger, Naomi Scheman, Mary Ellen Shaw, Al Sicherman, Bill Souder, Dan Sullivan, Mary Turck, Barbara Ungar, Shirley Ungar, and Peter Vaughan.

Jon Spayde's editorial advice was invaluable, as was the research assistance of Jules Inda and Julia Mickenberg.

Introduction

•——————•———————•———————•———————•

If life is like a box of chocolates, why have the pleasures of eating become so bittersweet? These days the proffered box of bonbons isn't just an invitation to sample life's unpredictable pleasures; it has become yet another battleground in the struggle between discipline and desire. "No, really, I shouldn't," is the predictable reply—and then you do.

When the snake enticed Eve in the Garden of Eden, the only food she was forbidden to eat was the apple. Today virtually every element of the American diet has become problematic for one reason or another. In the fifties it was sex that inspired feelings of guilt, anxiety, or shame; in the nineties it is food.

We have become a nation obsessed with eating. This preoccupation with food and diet isn't limited to the estimated thirty million Americans who are at risk for hunger and malnutrition, or to the estimated eight million Americans who suffer from anorexia and bulimia. Nor is it restricted to the estimated eighty million Americans who are clinically obese, or the nearly three out of four who are merely overweight. These statistics are merely evidence of an obsession with food so deeply embedded in our culture that it touches nearly every one of us.

This obsession manifests itself in the millions of men and women* who many times a day berate themselves for

---

* The reasons that issues such as diet and body image seem to affect women more than men will be explored in the course of this book. In essence, it is a consequence of differences in the ways in which our culture shapes women's and men's sense of identity.

xi

being too fat or eating too much, or who worry incessantly about whether their food is too rich in cholesterol, calories, salt, sugar, or saturated fat. Reduced-calorie food and beverages, formerly specialty foods for diabetics and dieters, have become staples of the American diet. We all (or nearly all) watch our weight these days, and we all watch ourselves. Doing so has become so much a part of our daily life that we hardly notice anything peculiar about it. It is, in short, as American as apple pie.

To foreign visitors this preoccupation with eating is one of the most striking features of our culture. It isn't only the prevalence of obesity that provokes their comments but also the omnipresence of food: the staggering selections in our supermarkets, the enormous size of restaurant portions, and the American habit of eating any time and any place—while driving in our cars, walking down the street, watching television, or talking on the phone. In fact, to help lure couch potatoes away from the TV set, theater owners have recently developed the cinema café, complete with waiters and tables in front of each row of seats, so that we can munch away on pizzas or hot dogs just like at home, without even having to get up to go to the refrigerator. A head designer for one of the Big Three automakers reports that customers seem to care more about cup holders than engine performance. "Why is it that people think they have to have a fifty-five-gallon barrel of Mountain Dew to drive to work?" he asks plaintively.

We seem to be eating more and more but enjoying it less and less. The pride many Americans once felt in producing the cheapest food in the world has given way to guilt over how it is produced: over the exploitation of farmworkers, the profligate use of pesticides and synthetic fertilizers, and the destruction of family farms, rural economies, and the natural environment.

But these kinds of guilt pale beside the shame we feel about our bodies and our eating habits and the fear and anxiety that we experience over the safety and wholesomeness of the foods we consume. Supermarket aisles and restaurant menus have become danger zones, as we worry about the health risks of cholesterol and saturated fat, sugar and sodium, salmonella and *E. coli*, and pesticides and antibiotics. A seemingly endless series of news reports about pesticides, hormones, and food poisonings leave us wondering whether *anything* is safe to eat.

As the norms of beauty and fitness projected by the media have become more stringent, the obsession with our bodies has intensified, going far beyond a prudent concern for our health and appearance. As we wrestle with our own weakness, our inability to keep our bodies under control, it takes on strong overtones of guilt and moral judgment. And the moral judgment isn't one we impose exclusively on ourselves; it is also a judgment that we make about others. To paraphrase Will Rogers, it's no sin to be fat, but it might as well be.

The Garden of Eating examines how we have come to find ourselves in this dire predicament and proposes what we can do to get out of it. The startling contradiction between the prodigious bounty of the American table and the unprecedented level of anxiety and prevalence of eating disorders suggests that food has taken on new and powerful meanings in our lives.

The idea that much compulsive eating is driven by an inner emptiness is hardly new, however. Diet gurus such as Geneen Roth, in books like *Feeding the Hungry Heart* and *When Food Is Love*, explore the links between overeating and an inner hunger. Far less attention is given to the cultural dimension of this problem: Why has there been such an explosive growth in eating disorders? Roth traces her own eating disorders to a physically abusive mother who was addicted to drugs and alcohol, and a father who was "often absent or emotionally unavailable." The larger puzzle is why

there are so many other men and women with similar stories to tell. What are the larger forces in the culture that produce these dysfunctional families and wounded children?
And why is eating the way we choose to treat these wounds?

This crisis of eating isn't happening in a vacuum. It's
happening at a time when nearly everything else in our culture seems to be drifting or falling apart, from our neighborhoods to our schools to our confidence in government, the
news media, and religious institutions. As we move from a
modern to a postmodern stage of development, everything
that once seemed solid now seems to melt into air. The
transformations that are taking place are undermining many
of the traditional sources from which Americans derived
their sense of identity, including their traditional eating
habits.

It is in the realm of food that this transformation affects
us at a gut level. At a time when so many of the other certainties of our lives are crumbling, the urge to turn to food
for security and nurturance intensifies. But when food itself
becomes threatening, the anxiety is intensified.

It wasn't always this way. There was a time, or so it
seems in retrospect, when eating was a simple pleasure, and
Americans tackled it with less sophistication—and more
gusto—than anyone else in the world. Steak was king of the
table, but there was always room for Jell-O. We'd open the
lunch box to find a bologna sandwich and a couple of Oreos,
and we were satisfied. If we weren't really living in a "garden
of eating," at least we had our innocence.

How did this loss of innocence come about? Something
happened, rather abruptly in the early sixties, right around
the time that Julia Child launched her television program,
"The French Chef." Before Child, food was simply something
we ate—with gusto but without angst. Since then it has
become a core element of our identity. The serpent offered
Eve a bite of the apple, and—having bitten into it—she and

Adam beheld their nakedness and felt shame. Child offered us a bite of tarte Tatin, coq au vin, and blanquette de veau, and—having tasted them—we looked at our Jell-O molds, tuna casseroles, and Hostess Twinkies and recoiled in shame.

In the aftermath of our seduction, we quickly discovered a whole world of sensory pleasures awaiting us. Travel to Europe exploded in the sixties, and so did the demand for formerly exotic "gourmet" foods. In a boom time for the American economy, Child gave Americans a permission to spend on foods that a few years earlier would have seemed snobbish or pretentious. Cooking was quickly seized on as a form of self-expression.

Once this new self-consciousness about food took hold, the rest was only a matter of time. Only after this climate had been established could Cesar Chavez seize the nation's moral imagination, showing us how the purchase of table grapes or iceberg lettuce could be a moral and political choice, or could Frances Moore Lappé make the same connection a few years later between our appetite for beef and the issues of hunger and environmental destruction.

It was also in the early sixties that the eroticization of food took hold of mass culture in unprecedented ways. When Tony Richardson's film *Tom Jones* appeared in 1963, its erotic feasting scene was regarded as a breakthrough. Today it's hard to turn on the television or open a magazine without encountering sensuous, glistening images of food—often enlisted in the marketing of such mundane merchandise as fast-food burgers and bottled salad dressings. A mound of whipped cream, a dewy bunch of grapes, a tawny turkey—food has become sexy, while sex has become problematic.

This transformation of our culture has had a powerful impact on how we think and talk about morality. As never before in American society, food has become eroticized, politicized, and invested with symbolism and moral power.

Today, while the old morality lies in shambles, a harsh new morality of the body reigns supreme. The word "sinful" is hardly ever used today except in connection with dessert. It would be wrong to dismiss this as mere metaphor: According to one recent study,[1] single women who have affairs with married men are generally untroubled by feelings of guilt; by contrast, many dieters feel powerful guilt and self-loathing after succumbing to the lure of Häagen-Dazs.

In part, guilt about food represents a shrinking of the realm of morality from a once-majestic kingdom to a beleaguered enclave. Psychologists have carved out much of the territory, persuading us that conduct we once called good or evil is better understood in terms of psychopathology. And though the war is still being fought, there has been a large popular uprising aimed at overthrowing the dominion of morality over our sexual lives. So why, at a time when morality is in retreat in almost every other sphere, has food become so morally problematic?

At the heart of this new food guilt is a migration of both our eroticism and our moral focus from our groins to our guts. There is, I grant, still plenty of moral anxiety about sexuality, but not nearly as much as there once was. In the Victorian era, when there was a more vibrant public world, the core of personal identity was thought to be found in how one connected to the social world—thus the tremendous emphasis on honor, duty, and above all, sex, that most intimate and defining connection.

Sex was therefore fraught with moral perils and intense drama; a sexual transgression was a threat against the social order. Today it's increasingly regarded as a private matter, largely because there is no social order in the old sense. It's of considerably less interest to everyone—including, often, the participants. As society has become more individualistic and private, we have learned to express and understand ourselves mostly in terms of what we consume. Small wonder, then, that eating has become more morally troublesome.

The increasing demands of the ideal body type promoted by the media are, of course, closely correlated to our guilt over eating. It's hard for most of us to eat three squares a day and still look like Cindy Crawford or Patrick Swayze. It's no coincidence that ever-more-emaciated models appeared in fashion ads simultaneously with the explosion in reported cases of bulimia and anorexia and a big boom in the diet book and diet food industries. While the rates of some eating disorders such as anorexia and bulimia may have stabilized or even declined slightly, they remain at very high levels, and obesity continues to increase.

It is striking that at the same time as our formal political freedoms have expanded, another kind of domination has tightened its grip, especially on the lives of women, a domination demanding the disciplining of the body. The success of the diet and exercise industries can be seen as a manifestation of that domination, as can the dramatic increase in eating disorders. Although feminists have waged war against the tyranny of slenderness, many Americans, and especially women, still live in the battle zone.

Is there a way out of this dilemma? Making peace with food begins with examining the role of food in our lives, and sorting out the psychological, cultural, and ethical factors that complicate that relationship. Identifying our core values and developing a consistent food ethic is one process that not only gives us a guide for action but also creates dimensions to our sense of self that go beyond our roles as consumers.

Guilt, long shunned as a destructive emotion, can play a very positive role in our lives, if we have a clear and consistent understanding of our own values, and a mature and discriminating conscience able to recognize when guilt is appropriate. To that end, it will be valuable to think seriously about such issues as animal rights and animal suffering, environmental destruction, and human exploitation. In addition to discussing these issues at a theoretical level, we can take practical steps to make food choices that reflect our values.

But making careful choices as consumers may not be enough to heal our troubled relationship with food, if its true source lies in a deeper kind of hunger: the hunger for meaning. To satisfy that hunger, we need to reach for sources of meaning and self-affirmation that lie beyond the role of consumer. If that kind of meaning seems to be in short supply in our consumer society, that may be precisely because it cannot be bought. But it can be cultivated, and if the soil in which it grows is carefully tended, it will flourish. Ultimately, to see the world as a garden is also to change how we see ourselves.

1

The Paradox of Plenty

The world is so full of a number of things,
I'm sure we should all be as happy as kings.
—ROBERT LOUIS STEVENSON

I can't get no satisfaction.
—MICK JAGGER

THE CORNUCOPIA

Considering the unprecedented bounty of the American food table, you'd think we'd all be as happy as kings. But we're not. In fact we're miserable. Richer than ever before, the American food experience is also more troubled. The revolutionary changes in American eating habits that began in the early 1960s have brought with them an era of unprecedented gastronomic hedonism, and paradoxically, an era of rampant food anxieties.

Call it the paradox of plenty.

The remarkable becomes commonplace so quickly that we scarcely notice how much, and how fast, the way we eat has changed. The range of food choices available to the American consumer today was simply unimaginable four decades ago. Our vocabularies have expanded to take in the names of foods and places that once seemed exotic: Szechuan and Tuscany, quiche and tagliatelle, potstickers and wasabi, chardonnay and gyros. Foods that were once seen only in the most exclusive restaurants are now available in supermarket freezer cases.

Nature may be indifferent to human suffering, but the American food industry—the vast network of food processors, marketers, technologists, and retailers—is keenly interested in our happiness. Every year the industry spends billions on research, manufacturing, marketing, and advertising, in a never-ending effort to find new ways to make us happy, or at least to make us spend. Each year the number of new products increases, and competition for shelf space becomes more intense.

Supermarkets now carry twelve times as many different products as they did in 1961—an average of thirty thousand items. In 1994 the number of new products and product-line extensions reached a record 21,262. It is estimated that as many as 94 percent of these new products will fail, but others will rise up endlessly to take their place.

The supermarket itself is a combatant in this Darwinian struggle, driven by the lash of competition constantly to seek new ways to make our lives more pleasurable. Supermarkets have gamely fought back against the growing rivalry from restaurants, gourmet shops, ethnic markets, food co-ops, health food stores, and fast-food chains by opening in-house delis and bakeries, offering bulk foods and organic produce, ethnic and specialty food sections, and espresso carts and juice bars. Nearly anything you can get at McDonald's or KFC can also be bought at the supermarket, from prescored burger patties and microwavable French fries to heat-and-serve chicken nuggets and extra-crispy "broasted" chicken. Many upscale supermarkets now even have their own restaurants on the premises.

An explosion of choice greets you in every aisle of the supermarket. The produce section has been set free from the tyranny of the seasons. Asparagus in January now seems as unremarkable as raspberries in November. In part that is because the produce market has become global. Apples from New Zealand or Argentina, red, yellow and purple peppers from Holland, grapes from Chile, and clementines from Morocco have become commonplace. A stroll through a typical midscale midwestern grocery store reveals a cornucopia of fresh foods that were unknown to most Americans a generation ago: fresh shiitake, enoki, oyster, and portobello mushrooms; kiwano melons and passionfruit; daikon radishes and salsify; fresh cilantro, chayote squash, and habanero peppers; and Oriental eggplants and tomatillos.

The experience of shopping saturates the senses. Fresh lettuces and vegetables, misted regularly by nozzles, shine in the bright light. Every aisle is a riot of color, each package eagerly clamoring for your attention. In supermarkets with in-store bakeries, the aroma of fresh-baked bread is vented throughout the premises, while demonstrators arouse the palate with samplings of sorbets, sausages, or salsas.

Stores that a generation ago carried fish either frozen into blocks or molded into fish sticks now have their own in-house fish markets, offering fresh tuna, trout, and salmon; raw and frozen shrimp; fresh oysters, clams, and scallops; and live lobsters. The freezer case is as cosmopolitan as the produce section. Chicken Kiev and chicken cordon bleu, once available only in the most elegant gourmet restaurants, now come plastic wrapped in individual six-ounce servings, ready to zap in the microwave. Convenience foods once meant Campbell's tomato soup and Swanson's TV dinners; today the choices range from Kung Pao shrimp to beef chimichangas to chicken parmigiana to infinity.

The fever of invention runs rampant as marketers end-lessly elaborate on the themes of our consumption, taking old products and making them new again by offering them in different sizes, different flavors, freeze-dried or frozen, low fat or high fiber, dealcoholized or decaffeinated, microwav-able or shelf stable, extra spicy and nacho-style. Whether it's shelf-stable cooked beets in a sealed-foil pouch that you hunger for, or refrigerated instant microwavable cheese omelettes in a cup, they're as close as the supermarket shelf.

If supermarkets are now full of foods that were once the sole province of gourmets, gourmets have ventured into gas-tronomic territory that the serious eaters of a previous gen-eration could scarcely have imagined. At upscale markets like Manhattan's Balducci's or Gourmet Garage, or their counterparts in other American cities, the shelves are stocked with arborio rice, walnut oil, buffalo mozzarella, and fresh quail eggs.

The old-style neighborhood bakery has largely van-ished, along with the neighborhood that supported it, but in more affluent communities, upscale bakeries are prolifer-ating, offering aromatic Italian focaccia and Parisian baguettes. The growing ethnic diversity of America's cities has also proved a boon for the serious eater: In most major metropolitan areas, you can now find Indian, Chinese, South-east Asian, Mexican, and Middle Eastern markets, offering everything from homemade Laotian papaya salad, steamed Vietnamese pork buns, and pickled Korean kimchi to fresh cactus pears, preserved duck eggs, and stuffed grape leaves; as supermarkets try to compete for customers, these prod-ucts are showing up on their shelves as well.

Coffee consumption has rebounded dramatically after three decades of steady decline, as Americans have rediscovered the pleasures of good java. The old neighborhood coffee shop, driven to virtual extinction by the proliferation of

golden arches, has made a comeback in many urban neighborhoods, albeit in the trendier form of the coffee bar,
offering espresso, capuccino, and attitude.

Restaurants have undergone the same transformation.
A generation ago middle-class families went to restaurants
for special occasions, and most meals were prepared at
home.[1] Outside of New York, Los Angeles, New Orleans, and
a few other large cities, restaurant dining in the fifties was
meat and potatoes, patty melts, and tuna salad sandwiches.
In 1961 Americans spent twenty-one cents of every food
dollar on restaurants, but by 1995 the figure had topped
fifty cents.

Much of that money is spent at fast-food restaurants,
which offer speed, convenience, and ever-expanding variety.
The drive-ins of the fifties, with their limited menus of
burgers, malts, shakes, and fries, were the fast-food restaurants of their generation, but they are painfully slow by
today's standards, set by the drive-through lanes of McDon-
alds and its competitors.

And as the fast-food wars have intensified, selection has
expanded. McDonald's now offers Chinese chicken salad,
chicken fajitas, and even McPizzas, while competitors ring
ever more imaginative changes on the constant themes of
fast-food cuisine: Frisco burgers on sourdough buns at
Hardee's, chicken fingers at Arby's, Caesar salads at
Wendy's. KFC met the late–eighties craze for crunchiness by
introducing a new extra-crispy version, and responded to
the concerns about health and fat by marketing Rotisserie
Gold birds in the nineties.

The French restaurants that flourished in the first blush
of the gourmet revolution, serving quiche and crepes, have
largely fallen by the wayside, superceded by waves of
Szechuan and Thai, Cajun and Carribean, Northern Italian
and Ethiopian. In Minneapolis–St. Paul, the most ethnically
homogeneous metropolitan area of its size in the United

States, the adventuresome eater has dozens of different cuisines to choose from, ranging from Afghan, Algerian, and Austrian, to Caribbean, Eritrean, and Korean, Laotian, Peruvian, Thai, Ukrainian, and Vietnamese.

Food has become as trendy as fashion: A vanguard of food adventurers discovers a new cuisine, and a flurry of magazine and newspaper articles popularizes it. As the new cuisine becomes more widely known, it is modified to meet tastes of a broader audience. By the time Kung Pao chicken and chicken mole make it to the supermarket freezer case, they may bear very little resemblance to the versions eaten on the streets of Chengdu or Guadalajara, but no matter. By then the restless vanguard has long since moved on to the next hot new cuisine.

The cutting edge of restaurant dining, though, is at the suburban malls and shopping centers, where chain operators like General Mills (the Olive Garden) and Carlson Companies (T.G.I. Friday's) pay top dollar for the combination of high-traffic location and high disposable income. And there the newest trend is toward offering fantasy dining experiences.

The foodie revolution has accelerated the pace of cross-cultural creativity, with results ranging from Mexican pizzas and frozen pizza rolls to Burger King's French and Italian chicken sandwiches. In fact the changes that these cuisines undergo transform them into something uniquely American. Long before the foodie revolution, the business of reinventing foreign foods for American tastes gave us such gastronomic neologisms as spaghetti and meatballs (virtually unknown in Italy), chop suey (invented in San Francisco), and that church cookbook classic "African chow mein" (comprising hamburger, chopped celery, canned chow mein noodles, and cream of mushroom soup).

But today the most discriminating diners want nothing to do with such lowbrow fare; they are on an endless quest for authenticity. The measure of authenticity is usually foreignness, how distant the foodstuff or dining experience seems from whatever is most American and familiar. Hence the eagerness with which sophisticated diners have embraced balsamic vinegar, porcini mushrooms, lemongrass, and sun-dried tomatoes. Choosing these foods gives a measure of the diners' own worldliness, and sets them apart from those less sophisticated Americans who might stumble over the pronunciation or hesitate at eating something so unfamiliar. The insistence on authenticity bespeaks higher standards; if you know what Italian cuisine is really supposed to taste like, then you have a level of awareness and judgment that sets you apart from most other diners. Buried inside the notion of authenticity is an undertone of contempt for the inauthenticity of mass culture.

At the more ambitious Italian restaurants, menu listings in Italian are de rigueur, and the more obscure the better. Now that fettucine Alfredo is available in the freezer case of the local supermarket, and is on the menu at T.G.I. Friday's, it's time for the serious eater to move on.

And the ground keeps shifting. Now that polenta has made its way into the refrigerator section of the local supermarket, it no longer can serve as a cultural marker; it is becoming déclassé. The adroit gourmet is sensitive to these changes, is able to gracefully make the transition from Chablis to chardonnay, and chardonnay to sauvignon blanc as each of these spreads in popularity to the mass market, without missing a beat.

But more than just class consciousness lies behind this constant trendiness; there is also a kind of nostalgia—a desire to live in another world. Dishes and restaurants described as authentic offer themselves as faithful re-creations of foods and establishments that existed in a happier and more secure time and place. New high-concept Italian restaurants, such as Tucci Bennuch and T.G.I. Friday's

Italianni's, adorn their menus with old family photographs, and feature family platters.

Of course, the foodie revolution has not affected everyone equally, and even many Americans whose eating habits have changed relatively little since the 1960s have been not been unaffected by it. A gastronomic elite has sailed off, evolving a food culture that differentiates it from the mass of American eaters, who have by and large remained loyal to the traditional American diet of green beans supreme and tuna-noodle casserole. If you still eat Spam and Jell-O, your diet hasn't changed, but your location on the social scale probably has.

We take for granted not only the variety of foods available to us but also the speed and convenience with which our food is available for consumption. Supermarkets stay open around the clock, and a whole new category of convenience stores has opened up for shoppers in too much of a hurry to wait in a checkout line. Fast-food drive-through lanes offer instant gratification into the wee hours of the morning.

Processed foods are one of the biggest growth areas in the supermarket, and have become so ubiquitous that we no longer give them a second thought. Frozen entrées and canned soups are nothing new, but added convenience has been processed into nearly every other department in the supermarket, from packages of skinless, boneless, pre-marinated chicken breasts and prestuffed pork chops to prepeeled and -sliced pineapples, prepared deli trays, and precooked racks of ribs.

The category of fun foods has also exploded. Humans have always taken pleasure in eating, but eating for fun is something different. Today the well-stocked supermarket has aisle after aisle of snack foods. New products like Screaming Yellow Zonkers, Pop Rocks, cheese curls, and taco chips are fun foods. So are soft drinks. Once an occasional soda fountain treat, soft drinks have become part of the daily diet for most Americans. In fact, our per capita consumption of soft drinks recently surpassed our consumption of tap water.

The supermarket shelves also reflect our growing concern with health. As the formerly marginal health food industry has grown, mainstream supermarkets have opened up entire sections stocked with organic produce, soy milk, organic tofu, and bulk food bins of granola and graham flour. The dairy section carries frozen yogurt and frozen tofu desserts alongside the premium and super-premium ice creams, 1 and 2 percent and skim milk, milk cultured with acidophilus bacteria for the lactose intolerant, and milk certified to be from cows not treated with bovine growth hormone.

As scientific research has deepened our understanding of the causes of heart disease, hypertension, and obesity, food technology has kept pace, giving us an ever-expanding list of reformulated foods—sugar-free soft drinks, fat-free mayonnaise, cholesterol-free cheeses and egg substitutes, fat-free luncheon meats, and many more. Concern about cholesterol and saturated fats has given rise to a whole market category of vegetable-oil spreads of varying degrees of softness, and such high-tech products as Olestra, a non-digestible fat, and Simplesse, a fat substitute.

For most of human history the work of procuring and preparing food has been arduous, and for much of the human population, it remains that to this day. Whatever the stresses of modern American life, the job of putting a meal on the table is far less difficult than it was for our ancestors, or than it is for the people—usually women—of the Second and Third Worlds, for whom the chores of hunting for firewood, pounding millet, hauling water, and tending smoky fires consume hours of every day.

New technology has also transformed the way we cook

and eat. Cooking, once one of the primary and defining tasks of the housewife, is increasingly becoming a hobby. Weekday meals aren't so much cooked as assembled—a dinner of fresh pasta from the dairy case topped with any one of dozens of brands of marinara sauce and accompanied by garlic bread, heated in the toaster oven.

Home appliances have evolved to make work in the kitchen easier, if not more rewarding. If you have a yen for homemade bread, electric baking machines make it as easy as adding a few ingredients and pressing a button or two; the mixing and kneading and baking are all done automatically. You no longer even have to combine the ingredients; prepackaged bread mixes are now available at the supermarket, for little more than the cost of a loaf of bread. For the ultimate in convenience, there is Hammacher Schlemmer's all-in-one breakfast center; "the only timer-controlled home appliance that wakes you up, brews coffee, toasts bread and prepares two perfect sunny-side-up eggs at the same time—all in just 10 minutes."

Early predictions that the microwave oven would transform the way we cook proved false; instead the invention of the microwave has created a vast new market for frozen and other prepared foods. The Cuisinart food processor and its less expensive knockoffs became a virtual necessity in middle-class homes as the cooking craze swept the United States in the early eighties; we needed it in order to make it easier to prepare at home those dishes we watched Julia Child prepare on television.

FAT-CITY BLUES

We are, in short, living in an eater's paradise—or at least an eater's fantasyland. Why, then, are so many of us so unhappy, so tormented about how we eat, what we eat, and above all, how much we eat? Our food choices may be richer than ever, but never before have we seen so much anxiety, guilt, fear, and shame around food and eating.

Before the mid-sixties, few Americans stopped to think about whether their tuna was dolphin-safe, their eggs came from free-range hens, or the workers who harvested their coffee were fairly compensated for their labor.

Today hardly an element in the American diet doesn't carry some moral stain. Bumper stickers remind us that meat is murder, and magazine ads confront us with gruesome pictures of anemic penned-up calves, brood sows chained to concrete slabs, hens stuffed into wire-mesh cages, downed cattle in slaughterhouses. We turn away but the images remain.

But the guilt that American consumers feel about the impact of their eating habits on the ecology of the planet or on animal welfare, and the concern they may feel about the living and working conditions of the people who grow and process their food, all pale in comparison with the shame and anxiety they feel about their own bodies.

This is particularly so for women. Psychologists Rosalyn Meadow and Lillie Weiss, who specialize in the treatment of women with eating disorders and/or sexual problems, have observed striking parallels between the constant agonizing that many women face today—"to eat or not to eat" and the dilemma of thirty years years ago—to "do it" or not to "do it." "Food has become a source of incredible anxiety for millions of women, simultaneously . . . an object of dread and of intense desire. Women are engaged in an ongoing battle with food: craving it, fearing it, and letting it control their lives. The battle between abstinence and self-indulgence is waged on a daily basis."[2]

Roam the aisles of a supermarket or the pages of a food magazine and you will find a veritable forest of moral messages embedded in the advertising and the packaging, from foods explicitly advertised as "guilt-free," such as fat-free desserts, to foods such as superrich premium ice creams and gourmet chocolates. The words are old but the meanings and the morality are new: This is a morality of the body, in which fat is bad and thin is good.

Food has come to occupy the place in our consciousness once held by sex. The inexorable link between sin and lust, between the forbidden and the desired, has replicated itself in our attitudes toward eating. It is in succumbing that we fulfill our desires, but to succumb is evil. Just as the medieval penitent struggled against the Satan within, the dieter is locked in eternal combat against the temptation that lurks within his or (usually) her soul.

The social meaning of corpulence differs from culture to culture. In some African and Polynesian cultures, obesity has traditionally been prized as a symbol of prosperity. And even in American society, corpulence has had different meanings and value over time. In the era of Diamond Jim Brady and Lillian Russell, corpulence was a sign of prosperity. But in our time fat carries not merely a social stigma, but a moral one. Fatness is the outward sign of an inward failing, a lack of self-control. Prejudice against fat people is one of the last remaining socially accepted bigotries. The most striking aspect of this hatred of fat people, in a society where a large majority of the population is overweight, is that the most common form of this hatred is self-hatred. Fat people who do manage to achieve a level of self-acceptance (that is, "fat pride") report being targets of particularly intense hostility: If they are fat, they ought at least to be ashamed of themselves.

But the problem is bigger than just obesity. An estimated 8 million Americans suffer from eating disorders, most notably anorexia (self-starvation), bulimia (a pattern of binge eating and vomiting), and compulsive eating. A recent Gallup poll reports that three out of four Americans worry about the health effects of their diet.

The human misery behind these numbers is palpable.

The countless magazine stories about weight loss and eating disorders may help fuel this food obsession, but surely they also reflect it. And the titles of best-selling books also give a clear indication of how troubled this relationship has become: *Making Peace with Food*, *When Food Is Love*, *Fat and Furious*, *Feeding the Hungry Heart*, and countless more.

A great deal of media attention has been focused on eating disorders, as they are commonly called. Calling them disorders suggests a departure from normalcy, but normalcy has disappeared from American eating, or rather, the normal state for most Americans is one of obsession with food. The statistics on percentages of Americans who have been diagnosed with eating disorders can be taken to imply that the rest of the population does not have problems with eating, but weight and body image issues are as much of a preoccupation for the men, and especially women, who manage to stay within the bell curve of normal weight as they are for those who have been given clinical labels. A poll of 33,000 women by *Glamour* magazine found that 75 percent considered themselves "too fat," even though only 25 percent were above insurance company ideal weight standards, and 30 percent were actually below.[3]

The obsession starts very early. In a study of fourth-grade girls, 90 percent were on some kind of diet.[4] In 1990, it was estimated that some 44 percent of high-school-aged girls and 15 percent of boys were on some kind of diet.[5] The diets don't help much; according to the Centers for Disease Control, obesity is growing faster among youth than among adults.

There is, of course, good reason to be skeptical about these sorts of statistics. Behind every such alarming set of numbers there is a veritable industry of people who have a vested interest in generating them, in labeling and medicalizing and pathologizing and ultimately treating varieties of human behavior that in other cultures might be seen in other terms.

As American waistlines expand, so does the sense of guilt and shame. Obesity has become a moral category, a measure of our character. Our obsession with weight and body images has created a weight-loss industry whose revenues are estimated to run between forty and fifty billion dollars a year, including expenditures on diet soft drinks, artificial sweeteners, fitness clubs, commercial and medical weight-loss programs and centers, low-calorie foods and diet foods, meal replacements, appetite suppressants, and diet books, cassettes, and videos. (The industry, in turn, spends billions every year promoting itself, filling the airwaves and the pages of magazines with messages about weight.)

What makes the figures especially remarkable is that hardly anyone actually accomplishes any long-term weight loss through diets or weight-loss programs. Four out of five clients of these programs lose no weight at all. Of those who do lose weight, only about one out of ten is able to keep the weight off for as long as two years.[6]

One might expect that the tremendous growth of low- and reduced-calorie foods would be reflected in a corresponding reduction in the average American waistline, as millions of Americans replaced their high-calorie foods with fat-free mayonnaise, low-fat yogurt and ice cream, and sugar-free Jell-O.

But just the opposite has happened. According to the latest statistics from the Centers for Disease Control, 58 million Americans—one out of every three adults—are now officially obese. Between 1963, the beginning of the foodie revolution, and 1980, obesity among preteens increased 54 percent, and extreme obesity (40 percent over ideal weight), increased 98 percent. A study of children of military personnel found that obesity nearly doubled between 1978 and 1990.[7] The switch to low-fat foods merely means that we can eat more. According to former Surgeon General C. Everett Koop, some three hundred thousand deaths annually are attributable to obesity.

The eating disorders in turn generate new opportunities for consumption: Psychotherapists, nutritionists, and weight-loss counselors of all stripes specialize in individual and group treatments for eating disorders. Even in the group setting, however, these therapies usually treat the disorder as a dysfunction of the individual, not the culture.

In addition to the anxieties we feel about our bodies, we are experiencing a growing concern about our diets. The eighties and nineties have seen a succession of eruptions of anxiety about the healthfulness and wholesomeness of the foods that we eat—first about sugar, then about salt, and more recently about fat, saturated fat, and cholesterol. Interspersed among these eruptions have been alarms about the dangers of various food preservatives, additives, and agricultural chemicals, ranging from MSG and saccharine to Alar and pesticide residues.

And never before has food seemed so dangerous. The Center for Science in the Public Interest (CSPI) mails out subscription appeals for its newsletter with a message on the envelope guaranteed to catch the attention of anxious eaters. "10 Foods You Should Never Eat . . ." it announces in large letters, with accompanying pictures of Campbell's Chicken Noodle Soup and a box of Quaker 100% Natural Oats and Honey Cereal.

Open the envelope, and you discover that Quaker cereal is "drenched with more artery-clogging fat than you'd get in a small McDonald's hamburger, and that half a can of Campbell's soup contains more than half your alloted quota of sodium for an entire day." But if these foods, a classic comfort food and a prototypical health food, aren't safe to eat, what is?

Of course, Campbell's Chicken Noodle Soup and Quaker 100% Natural Oats and Honey are both safe to eat. They are also, as the CSPI claims, too high in saturated fat and sodium, respectively, to be consumed frequently by the many Americans who already consume too much fat and salt. But the complete story about their nutritional value is perhaps a little too complex to fit onto the front of a fund-raising envelope, and when told in all its detail, it is likely to lose the sense of urgency that prompts anxious eaters to mail in subscription orders.

Every reassuring supermarket label carries an implicit threat. If "low-sodium," "fat-free," "all-natural," and "sugar-free" are good for you, what does that say about the rest of the foods in your grocery basket? Danger lurks at every turn, and the highly publicized nutrition studies contradict one another with such regularity that many Americans have begun to wonder whether anything is safe to eat.

It is virtually impossible to eat beef today without at least a passing thought to the issue of cholesterol and saturated fat. A growing number of Americans are swearing off red meat, some out of health concerns, others out of concerns about animal rights or the environmental damage caused by beef production. Others create their own compromises: They will eat beef but not veal, organically raised lamb but not pork, or poultry but not red meat.

Dairy products present us with many of the same anxieties: The cheese counter, freezer case, and dessert tray are packed with foods far richer and and more sensuous than anything we ever tasted thirty years ago, from high butterfat gourmet ice creams and triple-crème imported French Camemberts to New York–style cheesecakes. But these are sinful indulgences: For many Americans, it is impossible to enjoy a slice of cheesecake or a dish of Häagen-Dazs without a sense of transgression and a feeling of guilt or even self-loathing. They are at the same time tantalizing and dangerous.

This tension between appetite and desire has given rise to a vast new category of products designed to literally let us have our cake and eat it too: cheese substitutes made from soybean extracts, soft drinks made with artificial sweeteners, new ice creams made with high-tech fake fats, and fat-free imitation butter spreads, cream cheeses, and mayonnaises made with lists of ingredients that read like the stock inventory of a chemical company.

Even the produce section is not immune: We know that the reason that pile of Red Delicious apples looks so perfect is the abundant use of herbicides, pesticides, and synthetic fertilizers. The reassurances from government and industry about the safety of all of these chemicals are no longer as convincing as they once were: Even if the chemicals themselves won't poison us directly, there is a growing anxiety about the impact that all this tinkering will have in the long run on the delicate balance of nature.

But the dissatisfaction we feel about our food has yet another dimension: Despite all the bounty that's set down before us, deep down we don't find much of the food that we eat very satisfying. Although the menu has become considerably more elaborate, the food itself isn't very good. When older Americans complain that food doesn't seem to have as much flavor as it once did, the complaint is easily dismissed. After all, our taste buds become less sensitive as we grow older, and our memories rosier. But foreign visitors make the same sorts of remarks: Our vegetables seem lifeless, our poultry flavorless. By European standards, our bread, cheese, beer, coffee, and processed meats are insipid, lacking in texture, flavor, body, subtlety, character. Our processed foods are formulated to satisfy a mass market, and all wind up tasting a little bit similar, thanks perhaps to the ubiquitous presence of monosodium glutamate, hydrolized vegetable protein, salt, and disodium phosphate.

It is ironic that crusty breads, farmstead cheeses, craft-

brewed beers, coarsely textured sausages with natural cas-
ings—once the staples of daily life for even people of very
humble means—have all reappeared as specialty foods for
the luxury market. Their taste may be the same as in years
gone by, but their meaning is different. They are status symbols, tokens of class identity. Some products, especially the
microbrewery beers, have inspired clones like George Kil-
lian's, Samuel Adams, or Red Dog—mass-marketed consumer choices by which consumers can express their
repudiation of the role of mass-market consumer.

The same dissatisfaction we feel about the processed
foods in our diet extends to less processed foods, like produce, meat, and eggs. The growth of the produce section is
in part a response to our hunger for more natural, less
processed foods, but deep down we know that those perfect Red Delicious apples are hardly more "natural" than
frozen spaghetti dinners. Winter tomatoes are the most
notorious example: Genetically engineered, chemically fer-
tilized, mechanically harvested, gas-"ripened," they are as
much a manufactured product as Jell-O. And whatever joy
we may find in Jell-O, these tomatoes have a different standard of comparison. For anyone who has ever tasted a vine-
ripened summer tomato, these tomatoes simply don't taste
very good—nor do those perfectly shaped shiny Red Delicious apples, engineered for looks and shelf life but not for
flavor.

Herbert Hoover's promise of a chicken in every pot
dates back to a time when a stewing chicken on Sunday
symbolized a level of prosperity that many Americans could
only dream of. Today chicken is everyday fare, preferred
over beef because it is lower in fat, calories, and cholesterol.
While beef consumption has undergone decades of decline,
a trend that has only recently begun to reverse itself,
chicken consumption has increased dramatically in the past
two decades. Selective breeding and modern production

techniques have cut in half the time it takes to raise a chicken (from fourteen weeks to seven), and drastically cut the costs of production. Herbert Hoover's promise has been fulfilled, but it has proved to be empty: This skinless, boneless chicken is virtually flavorless.

It was long ago discovered that feeding livestock subtherapeutic doses of antibiotics increases food conversion efficiency. In the long term, however, this practice is accelerating the evolution of new strains of drug-resistant pathogens that will render the current generation of antibiotics ineffective.

The lack of flavor in the staple foods of the American diet seems like an unfortunate by-product of the development of food processing, but from the point of view of the food industry, it may not be so unfortunate at all. Food scientists tell us that we have a physiological mechanism called the appestat, which tells us to stop eating when we have received a sufficient amount of flavor. The less flavor satisfaction we obtain per mouthful, the more we must consume. Dr. Susan Schiffman of Duke University has also speculated that one reason for widespread obesity is the blandness of processed foods.[8]

Brewmasters discovered long ago this inverse relationship between body and flavor on the one hand, and the quality they call drinkability, the ease with which a product can be drunk in quantity, on the other. Progressively over the decades, to increase drinkability, the body, flavor, and alcohol content of the mass-marketed beers have been reduced. The television commercials of the 1980s, in which famous athletes and sports fans argued over whether they chose Miller Lite because of its great taste or because it was less filling, were a bit disingenuous on this score; Miller Lite is less filling than standard American beers because it has less of the hops that give beer its characteristic flavor and fewer of the nonfermentable sugars called maltodextrins that give beer body and the quality called "mouthfeel." It's also slightly lower in alcohol than regular beers, so one must drink more to achieve the same altered state of consciousness that can be achieved with fewer bottles of fuller-bodied beers. Needless to say, this translates into higher profits for the industry.*

Drunk at the recommended temperature, even the fuller-bodied American beers, like Budweiser and Miller Genuine Draft, have so little in the way of distinguishing flavor characteristics that in blindfold tests, most beer drinkers cannot identify their favorite brand. Since the nationally advertised brands all taste essentially the same, the advertisers' key strategy to create product differentiation in the minds of their consumers centers on creating positive associations with the product, associations that usually have more to do with the consumers' self-image than with the intrinsic flavor properties of the product.

So we are left with dissatisfaction, suspicion, and an unhappy palate. Jaded by advertising and packaging, we're used to being disappointed by the fact that the actual processed food never looks as good as the picture on the package, never tastes as good as the advertising promises.

Another remarkable aspect of our relationship to food is that although we are passionate, even obsessed about food, most Americans know very little about how their food is produced. The knowledge that we do have is repressed, and all the more powerful for that. The reality of how our food is produced conflicts sharply with a deeply cherished mythology.

At the same time that the traditional farm has virtually

---

* This process of maximizing profits by diluting the essential properties of the product is not unique to the brewing industry; the advent of cigarettes low in tar and nicotine has proved to be a similar boon to the tobacco industry, as addicted smokers must smoke more cigarettes to achieve the same level of nicotine in their bloodstreams.

disappeared from the American landscape, its imagery is everywhere in the American supermarket. Kraft, now a division of the diversified multinational Philip Morris, runs television commercials that hark back to the days when the company's founder sold his cheeses from a horsecart. Green Giant, now a subsidiary of Pillsbury, has moved most of its vegetable production to Mexico but still relies on the imagery of goodness "from the valley."

Animal husbandry practices have changed more dramatically in the last four decades than in any other time in American history. Once integrated into the farm economy as sources of labor and fertilizer as well as food, most of the approximately eight billion cattle, chickens, turkeys, and swine that are slaughtered every year in the United States spend their entire lives in confinement systems in which every element of their lives, from their sleep cycles to their reproduction, is controlled with an eye to maximizing profits. It isn't just the way we raise animals that has changed but the very body types of the animals themselves. The pig, once bred for lard, has been streamlined through selective breeding into a leaner, meatier animal. One experiment in genetic engineering even produced a pig with some human genes. Nature has become plastic, infinitely manipulable.

Although we cling to pastoral images of farming, and raise our children on the mythology of Old McDonald and Farmer Brown, the realities of factory farming are vastly different. While the term "factory farming" is usually used pejoratively, it is an accurate description of the way in which most of the food that most Americans consume is produced. The processes of tilling, planting, fertilizing, and harvesting grains and produce have been mechanized and, to an increasing degree, automated.

We have developed a profoundly ambivalent relationship to this new food technology. On the one hand, we have come to take the benefits of this technology for granted: We have evolved a lifestyle centered on the convenience of processed food, and the low prices of food produced by the use of herbicides, pesticides, mechanized farming, and genetic engineering.

And yet, on the other hand, there is something about the brave new world that food technology has brought us that is very frightening. Every news report of genetically altered frost-resistant strawberries or rot-resistant tomatoes stirs fears that our scientists, for all their confidence, are really only sorcerer's apprentices, unleashing forces on the world that they are powerless to control and whose consequences they cannot predict.

Only a relative handful of plant ecologists and environmental activists spend much time worrying about the potentials for ecological catastrophe posed by the new food technologies, but beyond the practical concern about large-scale natural disaster, many Americans share a pervasive, visceral sense of loss.

These feelings of anxiety and guilt about food are especially painful because of the place and meaning that food has in our lives. Beyond the simple biological fact that we must eat in order to survive, food is also a source of psychological comfort and nurturance. In times of great anxiety, we want to turn to food for comfort, and we find that, instead, food becomes yet another source of anxiety, guilt, fear, and distress. People respond to this dilemma in different ways: some by eating more, some by becoming more anxious, others by trying to find a relationship to food that can be a source of meaning.

The paradox of plenty poses a riddle about our culture, and ultimately about ourselves. To solve that riddle we must look more closely at our history, and at the ways in which our identities and desires are shaped by the larger forces in our culture.

2

The Foodie Revolution

We are in the midst of an extraordinary revolution today, this minute—a social revolution that is making astonishing, radical changes in how we live now, and how we live in the future.

—Cookbook author Irena Chalmers, writing in 1986

Something happened, rather suddenly, beginning in the early 1960s. French cuisine came into vogue in the United States. Millions of American homemakers, who had just made Peg Bracken's *The I Hate to Cook Book* a bestseller, rushed out in droves to buy *Mastering the Art of French Cooking,* by Julia Child, Simone Beck, and Louisette Bertholle. By the early seventies, cooking schools had opened all over the country, and in the decade that followed a new generation of gastronomic superstars became household names—in addition to Julia Child there were Jacques Pépin, Marcella Hazan, and Pierre Franey. Gourmet shops opened, selling everything from sun-dried tomatoes and stone-ground mustards to wild mushrooms and imported cheeses. The restaurant scene exploded.

There is little agreement over the meaning or causes of this transformation. But the changes are so sweeping that it has become commonplace to call it a revolution. This revolution has transformed not only the way we eat and the way we think about food but ultimately also the way we think about ourselves.

The transformation of what Americans ate brought with it a new set of attitudes, in which food became increasingly a marker for personal identity. As our attitudes about food have become more sophisticated, we have also become more self-conscious, an outlook that has given everything on the American plate a new dimension of meaning.

Although much attention has been focused on the gourmet revolution, it is the most visible part of a sweeping transformation in our lives as eaters that began in the early sixties. It was also in the sixties that the first signs of our current obsessions with eating and dieting emerged, as well as our anxieties over the wholesomeness and healthfulness of our diet and food supply.

While some eaters decamped in the direction of quiche, coq au vin, and osso buco, another segment embraced tofu, bean sprouts, yogurt, and granola. This was never simply a health food movement, though; food was understood in a political and moral context. As the antiwar movement grew, many activists began to articulate a connection between resisting the processed products of the corporate giants that dominate the food industry and resisting capitalism and imperialism.

A whole set of moral issues surrounding food came to public consciousness on an unprecedented scale, including the issues of cruelty to animals, environmental destruction, and the exploitation of farm workers at home and in the Third World. Michael Harrington's *The Other America* (1962) awakened Americans to the existence of widespread poverty in the midst of affluence. Though not entirely new, many of these issues burst into public consciousness with unprecedented force beginning in the sixties, after a long period of domestic tranquillity during which the majority of Americans had untroubled confidence in the assurances of the established food authorities: food scientists, nutritionists, and food inspectors.

The grape boycott of the mid-sixties, led by Cesar Chavez and the United Farm Workers, tapped into the spirit and energy of the civil rights movement by making the connection between consumer choices and social justice. Although the grape boycott (a subsequent boycott targeted lettuce) focused on only one product, it was only a matter of time before others made the connection more broadly. Other food boycotts were to follow: veal (animal cruelty), tuna (dolphins killed in fishing nets), foods and wines from South Africa (apartheid), and products made by Nestlé (for marketing infant formula in Third World countries).

Cookbook authors such as Mollie Katzen (*The Moosewood Cookbook*) and Frances Moore Lappé offered not only vegetarian recipes but also a vision of a way of life in harmony with the environment. In *Diet for a Small Planet* (1971), Lappé made explicit the link between individual food choices and global food issues: "What we eat is within our control, yet the act ties us to the economic, political and ecological order of our whole planet," Lappé told her readers.

Lappé's book stressed the connection between the American diet, rich in grain-fed meat, and hunger in the Third World. It takes sixteen pounds of grain to produce one pound of beef, Lappé informed her readers. And for every calorie of beef produced in feedlots, we burn seventy-eight calories of fossil fuel.

Weight and dieting had received relatively little attention from the media or the medical community in the early fifties, but starting later in the decade, articles about dieting became a staple of women's magazines. Starting in the sixties and continuing to the present, a succession of fad diets swept the country, propelled by bestselling books, including

Dr. Atkins' Diet Revolution, which taught millions of Americans how to lose weight rapidly by inducing ketosis, the inability to metabolize fat; Dr. Herman Tarnower's *Scarsdale Diet*; the *Beverly Hills Diet*; and countless others.

The ideal body type for women underwent a dramatic transformation, as the voluptuousness of Jane Russell, Marilyn Monroe, and Jayne Mansfield was replaced by the emaciated boyish look of British high-fashion model Twiggy and Jean Shrimpton and a new generation of more slender film stars. Paradoxically, as the ideal body type became increasingly slender, average body weight increased. The body continues to undergo redefinition, first lean and muscular, now the odd combination of narrow hips, flat stomach, and prominent cleavage.

The early sixties also saw the founding of Weight Watchers, one of the earliest pioneers in what has become a fifty-billion-dollar diet industry. Anorexia and bulimia, medical rarities in the first half of the century, became increasingly common. As obesity became medicalized, a series of medical procedures came into vogue as "treatment," including stomach stapling, jaw wiring, and, most recently, liposuction.

A gastronomic purification swept through the cooking world, as newspaper editors began to censor their columns and publishing houses their cookbooks, removing recipes that called for cream of mushroom soup, canned onion rings, Jell-O, or Lipton's Onion Soup Mix.

Not everyone followed this ban, however—such recipes continued to appear in small-town newspapers and church cookbooks, but they became one of the marks of the fissure that began to appear in American eating, between those people who were becoming part of the new consumer culture and those who remained behind.

Although not everyone participated directly in this revolution, nearly everyone has been affected by its larger consequences. Those whose diets did not change in the years of the revolution now have a class identity and social status they didn't have previously. The outbreak of this revolution signaled the breakdown of what had been a common food culture—a standard diet that nearly all Americans embraced or at least aspired to as they left behind their immigrant roots. What has emerged in its aftermath is what historian Warren Belasco has called "the two taste cultures."[1]

The job of reshaping public tastes fell largely to food writers and restaurant critics. The venerable *Gourmet* magazine was joined by a host of new glossies, including *Bon Appétit, Cuisine,* and *Food & Wine,* all with editorial content designed to complement the sophisticated lifestyle depicted in the advertising. In the fifties a popular local restaurant might have rated a passing mention in the newspaper's society column, in a report of who was seen with whom. By the seventies the society column had begun to disappear from newspapers, but restaurant reviews were becoming increasingly common. The food, not the company, was the main event this time around. Wine writers and food critics taught their readers a new vocabulary and new ways of looking at food and wine.

The early enthusiasm for the foodie revolution has by now given way to a questioning of its gains, a more sober reckoning of its losses, and, for many, a foreboding sense that rather than having broken our shackles, we have opened Pandora's box. "The food we eat and the water we drink are no longer the pure sources of nourishment and pleasure they once were," lamented David Steinman in *Diet for a Poisoned Planet* (Harmony Books, New York, 1990).[2] The fifties, formerly recalled as an era of sexual repression, stifling conformity, and the ever-present threat of nuclear annihilation, are reconstructed as paradise lost—the time of sock hops, innocent teen angst, quiet domesticity, and

Little League baseball. Red meat was king, and few Americans were troubled by concerns over calories, cholesterol, heart disease, or animal cruelty.

A veritable nostalgia industry has arisen around the fifties as the time before everything started to go so badly wrong, food—and otherwise. Hollywood's rosy re-creations of the time, in movies like *Peggy Sue Got Married* and television shows like *Happy Days*, have their gastronomic counterpart in the renewed popularity of retro diners, where the menu features meatloaf and mashed potatoes, malts, and macaroni and cheese.

These two different versions of the past are reflected in our strikingly ambivalent attitudes toward the foods of the fifties: on the one hand a patronizing contempt for the unsophisticated palates of the fifties, for the cuisine of hamburgers, fish sticks, and Jell-O, an unstated tone of smugness in our knowledge that at least when it comes to matters of taste, we are our parents' superiors. And on the other a sentimental embrace of "comfort food"—of meatloaf that is no longer merely meatloaf but the symbol of a less complicated, more innocent, and happier time.

No one captures this odd combination of affection and condescension more skillfully than the husband-and-wife team of Michael and Jane Stern, in such works as *Square Meals* (1984) and *American Gourmet* (1991). "We have become a gastronomically sophisticated country, but we should not discard favorite dishes because they are out of fashion," the Sterns advise their readers in the preface to *Square Meals*. "No matter how corny they seem to our newly refined sensibilities, there is nothing embarassing about a homely meat loaf or old-fashioned devil's food cake."[3]

DATING THE REVOLUTION

Craig Claiborne, retired food writer for the *New York Times*, said the foodie revolution began on June 17, 1947, the date of the first scheduled Pan Am round-the-world flight. Altho foreign travel certainly played an important role in the tra formation of American tastes, this date seems too early. As more and more Americans began to travel overseas in the years after World War II, their tastes became more sophisticated. But it was still a very long time before the pace of change accelerated to the point where it could truly be called revolutionary, or became so widespread that it really affected the eating habits of average Americans.

A stronger case can be made for January 1961, when Jackie and John F. Kennedy took up residency in the White House. President Truman's favorite fare had been roast beef and mashed potatoes, prepared by the housekeeper he and his wife, Bess, brought with them to Washington from Independence, Missouri. President Eisenhower preferred thick steaks and hash, and liked to eat from a tray while watching television. The Kennedys brought into the White House a real French chef, René Verdon, and an aura of glamour and sophistication. But this was the cuisine of Camelot, not everyday fare for the home cook.

The real beginning of the revolution came in 1962, with the first broadcast of Julia Child's television show, *The French Chef.* More than any other single individual, Julia Child brought gourmet foods into the American mainstream. Gourmet cooks and cookbooks existed long before Julia Child arrived on the scene, as did elegant French restaurants, but before Julia, French cuisine simply wasn't something that normal people ate.

Before Julia the gourmet was an odd fellow, effete, a bit of a snob, and almost always a bachelor. In fiction the best-known gourmet was the orchid-growing private detective Nero Wolfe, while in real life, America's most celebrated gourmets were James Beard and traveling salesman Duncan Hines. Women were banned from most of the more exclusive eating societies of the prewar era; whereas everyday cooking was woman's work, gastronomy was a man's pleasure.

Of course real men wouldn't touch such stuff. If the average American housewife had served blanquette de veau for dinner in the fifties, her husband and the kids would probably have refused to eat it. And if her husband had accepted it without at least some grumbling about being a meat-and-potatoes man, his very masculinity might have been suspect. To serve such fare to company, moreover, would have raised suspicions of pretentiousness.

Until Julia Child, French cuisine, like French culture, occupied a special place in the American social imagination. It represented the exotic, the sinful, or at least the naughty. A well-chaperoned college semester overseas, a trip to New York to see the cancan, dinner at a French restaurant.

Bourbon Street in New Orleans, where French cuisine flourished, was the capital of this Francophile culture, but every city of a certain size had its Allée Pigalle or Gay Paree nightclub, where for a two-drink minimum, one could have a measured taste of sin, a fleeting glimpse of the forbidden. Of the handful of French foods that entered into the American vocabulary before the gastronomic revolution of the sixties, it is worth contemplating why escargots Bourguignonne became such an object of particular fascination.

After Julia all that changed. Child's public television series, *The French Chef*, first aired on WGBH in Boston in 1962, was an immediate success, and made her cookbook, *Mastering the Art of French Cooking,* an instant bestseller.

A flood of cookbooks, cooking schools, and other cooking shows followed. Graham Kerr duplicated Julia Child's success on public television with a commercial television hit, *The Galloping Gourmet.* By 1968, when Time-Life launched its Foods of the World series, three of the top ten best-selling books were cookbooks. The speed with which American eating habits changed in the years that followed suggest the pent-up energy of a dammed river, bursting through walls that could no longer contain its energy. But where did this new force come from, and what had held it back?

In the fifties most Americans ate a very similar diet, regardless of socioeconomic class. For decades the favorite American foods, as indicated in a variety of surveys, were literally meat (steak or roast beef) and potatoes. In a 1947 Gallup poll, when Americans were asked what their favorite meal would be if money were no object, the top menu started with fruit or shrimp cocktail, followed by vegetable soup or chicken broth, steak with mashed or french-fried potatoes, peas, vegetable salad, rolls and butter, and apple pie à la mode for dessert.[4]

"The weekday dinner table at a corporate lawyer's household in upper-middle-class Flossmoor, Illinois, looked little different from an insurance company clerk's in Levit-town, New York," asserts food historian Harvey Levenstein. "Campbell's canned or Lipton's dried soup, broiled meat, frozen french fries, and a frozen green vegetable, with supermarket ice cream or a Jell-O concoction for dessert— an all-American 'square meal.'" Popular dishes such as tuna-and-noodle casseroles transcended class lines.[5]

You and Your Family's Food, a publication of the Bureau of Human Nutrition and Home Economics of the U.S. Department of Agriculture, offered recipes for standbys and special dishes, designed to help the homemaker who is "trying to do a blue-ribbon job of feeding a family well."[6]

There is little trace of the current anxieties about nutrition or food safety. The section of the book titled "Nutrition Up-to-Date . . . Up to You" is most striking for what it does not say. Cholesterol is not even mentioned, and the connections between diet and the diseases of affluence are barely mentioned. "You get top-rating proteins in foods from animal sources, as in meat, poultry, fish, eggs, milk, cheese. Some of these protein foods are needed every day; and it is an advantage to include some in every meal."

Very little is said about fat; the book merely advises that "Up to 35 years of age, if you can't be just right in weight, it is better to be plump than skinny. Beyond 35, excess fat becomes a greater health liability than thinness. Ills such as high blood pressure and kidney ailments are more common among overweights."

The developers of the recipes for *You and Your Family's Food*, which range from pot roast of beef and ham croquettes to corn pudding and pineapple-cottage-cheese mold, evidently took great care to ensure that none of their offerings would cause the unsuspecting eater to be overcome by uncontrollable passions. What is most striking about the recipes in this collection is the almost complete absence of any seasoning beyond salt and pepper. There is one recipe for curried meat that calls for two tablespoons of curry powder; to make a chop suey instead, you simply omit the curry powder and substitute either chopped almonds or sliced radishes and serve over crisp noodles.

At the beginning of the decade, most homemakers prepared these dinners from scratch. But the biggest innovation brought by the fifties was a dramatic increase in convenience foods. Frozen foods had been around since the twenties, but it was only in the fifties, after the Great Depression and the war years had stalled the market for freezers in homes and food markets, that they took off.

Cookbooks of the era show that the new processed foods were embraced with enthusiasm and considerable creativity. It was a time of innocence and confidence, when the United States was on top of the world and our pride in technology extended to the kitchen. America's unique contribution to global food culture is technological; we gave the world frozen food, Jell-O, TV dinners, and tomato-soup cake. Although it is commonplace today for gastronomic sophisticates to sneer at these inventions (and indirectly at the large portion of the American public that still eats this sort of fare), tremendous creativity went into concocting such fifties classics as chow mein, made with hamburger, cream of mushroom soup, chicken-rice soup, Minute Rice, soy sauce, and celery, or a "World's Best Meat Loaf," made with ground beef, Miracle Whip, chopped, sautéed onion, and bread crumbs, baked in a ring mold.

Midway into the American century, we had the imagination and the culinary self-confidence to create a whole new cuisine out of such high-tech bounty. Nature has never devised anything quite as colorful as Crown Jewel dessert, made of four different colors of Jell-O. The Swiss may have invented fondue, but, slaves to tradition, they never dared depart from Gruyère and Emmentaler or hot oil; only in the United States could fondue be made with canned condensed Cheddar cheese soup.

In part, this cuisine was a celebration of the modern. *The Jetsons*, for a time one of the most popular shows on television, offered a cartoon image of the direction in which American progress might someday lead: Judy's household chores have become effortless, thanks to a dazzling array of convenience foods and labor-saving devices. And thanks to the wonders of technology, a foretaste of this exciting new future was already available on supermarket shelves: Mom could mix up some Tang, the same drink enjoyed by the astronauts. The new cuisine was not without its erotic sub-text: where else on earth could one find a dish to rival the unabashed eroticism of "Candlelight Salad": a transected banana standing erect in a canned pineapple ring, topped with a dollop of Miracle Whip and a maraschino cherry?

The ideal of America as a classless society has never been more than a myth, but it has exercised a powerful influence on our sense of justice, our shared values, and our tastes. The New Deal, which opened the doors to the middle class for millions of working-class Americans, came not only in response to an economic depression but also in response to a period of great social instability.

The booming industrial economy reduced the economic distinctions between the working class and the middle class, and in our period of greatest cultural optimism, it seemed likely that the availability of higher education would, over the course of a generation, eliminate the cultural distinctions as well. The need for social solidarity in World War II further strengthened the ideal of a classless society: Wartime propaganda stressed that we were all in this struggle together and emphasized the dignity and worth of every citizen by contrasting them with the fascist, antidemocratic visions of the "master race." The war also strengthened another current of the prevailing values system: the emphasis on frugality and modesty.

A social contract prevailed, albeit uneasily, among the classes. The middle class was held out as the ideal, and although not everyone achieved that status, nearly everyone aspired to it. There was much grumbling about conformity and the pressure to keep up with the Joneses, but there was also a widespread contempt for "snobs"— people who chose a lifestyle that set them apart from the mass of their neighbors. Writing in the early fifties, popular southern author MacKinlay Kantor proudly proclaimed that he would rather eat his plain old flour-and-milk gravy "than any esoteric *sauce supreme* contrived by some third-generation hireling of the original Escoffier, who may be able to enchant sophisticates with his *Foie de Veau Poêle à la Bourgeoise* but who wouldn't know how to cook a meat loaf with browned potatoes if the entire fate of the Thursday night church supper of the Berean Guild depended on it."[7]

A social contract also prevailed between men and women in the fifties. Men were expected to marry and to support a family with their earnings. A woman's place was in the home, where she was responsible for cooking, cleaning, and child care.

This was the era of unsurpassed American self-confidence. A few years earlier, Henry Luce had proclaimed this the American Century, and a backward glance showed the United States on a winning streak: victorious in two world wars and now enjoying an unprecedented prosperity. Although the Cold War brought with it anxieties about nuclear destruction, most Americans were buoyed by the certainty that we were the good guys, and we were winning. The Cold War was framed as a moral struggle, one that demanded that we all be strong and work hard, and that just as our scientists had harnessed the energy of nature to create the atom bomb, the work of food scientists in the laboratories was harnessing the energies and resources of nature to the betterment of human life.

Previous eras had been marked by food fads and food safety scandals. But by the 1950s, a moral order had finally been imposed on the world of food. The Food and Drug Administration (FDA) guaranteed the wholesomeness of foodstuffs, and a national network of food scientists and dieticians spread a gospel of scientific nutrition. The job of teaching healthy nutrition was turned over to the American Dairy Council, which spread the gospel of the four food groups. (In retrospect it seems a bit odd that one of the four basic food groups should be the lactation products of an unrelated species, to which a large portion of the world's population is allergic.)

"Nutrition is the science that deals with food at work—food on the job for you," advised *You . . . and Your Family's Food.* "Modern knowledge of food at work brings a new kind of mastery over life. When you—and your family—eat the right food, it does far more than just keep you alive and going. The right food helps you to be at your best in health and vitality."

After the war a barrage of cultural propaganda urged women to stay at home and seek happiness as wives and homemakers. While boys took shop classes, girls studied home economics, where they learned to sew pink cotton hostess aprons and make carrot-and-raisin salad.[8] Gender roles were sharply differentiated, but at least as first, the work that women did in the home was valorized as vital to the health of the family and the security of the nation.

The image of domestic tranquillity was the self-image of the era, and during the fifties, few spoke out to challenge it. But beneath the surface pressures were building. In 1962, when Julia Child began her television program, only a year after the publication of volume 1 of *Mastering the Art of French Cooking*, another landmark book became an instant bestseller: Betty Friedan's *The Feminine Mystique*.

Friedan wrote of "a strange stirring, a sense of dissatis-faction, a yearning that women suffered in the middle of the twentieth century in the United States. Each suburban wife struggled with it alone. As she made the beds, shopped for groceries, matched slipcover material, ate peanut butter sandwiches with her children, chauffeured Cub Scouts and Brownies, lay beside her husband at night—she was afraid to ask even of herself the silent question—'Is this all?' "[9]

Although the women's magazines of the time held forth the image of women finding fulfillment in their role as full-time homemakers, this role was neither very satisfying nor, for many working- or middle-class households, very real-istic: The number of women working outside the home increased steadily throughout the fifties.

Technological and economic changes were rendering their roles as homemakers marginal. A succession of labor-saving devices, as they gave women the leisure to ask themselves "Is this all?", also undermined the perceived value of women's contributions to the household. The refrigerator and freezer changed the daily shopping trip into a weekly one. The dishwasher, the washing machine, and the dryer all contributed to a "de-skilling" of the American homemaker.

But most important was the transferral of food processing from the kitchen to the factory. Food producers found that it wasn't possible to get Americans to eat more food; to increase profits they would have to produce food more efficiently or build more value into their products: that is, make them more convenient. The 1950s brought not only the notorious TV dinner but also a whole cupboard of processed foods: instant mashed potatoes, instant rice, and instant cake mixes.

Advertisements for the new convenience foods saturated the popular culture of the day. With women's magazines heavily dependent on advertising from food manufacturers, food editors were under considerable pressure to create and publish recipes that offered new uses for these products.

The processed products were received with great enthusiasm. "It is understood that when you hate to cook, you buy already-prepared foods as often as you can," wrote Peg Bracken in the bestseller, *The I Hate to Cook Book*:

> You buy frozen things and ready-mix things, as well as pizzas from the pizza man and chicken pies from the chicken pie lady.
>
> But let us amend that statement. Let us say, instead, that you buy these things as often as you dare, for right here you usually run into a problem with the basic male. The average man doesn't care much for the frozen-food department, nor for the pizza man, nor for the chicken pie lady. He wants to see you knead that bread and tote that bale, before you go down cellar to make the soap. This is known as Woman's Burden.[10]

By 1962 the president of the Grocery Manufacturers Association could boast that convenience foods had cut the time that housewives had to spend in the kitchen from five and a half to one and a half hours. His numbers may be exaggerated, but by 1959, when Nixon held his famous kitchen debate with Krushchev, the domain of the American housewife was a far different place than it had been a mere two decades earlier.

The transfer of food production from the home to the factory, where foods had to be purchased with the income earned primarily by men, marginalized the role of women in the household economy and undermined the prevailing social contract. A 1963 article in *Playboy* mocked housework as "an easy low-pressure job that will permit you to spend most of each and every day as you please—relaxing, watching TV, playing cards, socializing with friends!!!"*

What emerged, to an unprecedented degree, was what Barbara Ehrenreich has termed an "asymmetry of need." What kept the social contract in place in the face of this asymmetry, she explains, were the strong social pressures on men to enter into the bonds of matrimony and assume roles and responsibilities as breadwinners. Men who resisted the pressure to marry and start a family were, according to the prevailing wisdom of the time, stigmatized as "mama's boys" or "not the marrying kind."

But by the end of the 1950s, as the domestic work of

---

* Quoted in Barbara Ehrenreich, *The Hearts of Men*, p. 48. (This echoes sentiments expressed as far back as 1877, when the editor of the *Stillwater* (Minn.) *Gazette* opined: "Now they have got canned Boston baked beans for sale at the groceries. If they keep on canning new things for the table, pretty soon a man will not need to get married at all. He can rent a room, buy a can opener, can live on the fat of the land, with a dog to lick off the plates." Cited in Marjorie Kreidberg, *Food on the Frontier: Minnesota Cooking from 1850 to 1900, with Selected Recipes* (St. Paul: Minnesota Historical Society, 1975), p. 30.

women became marginalized, those pressures weakened. Ehrenreich argues that one of the key figures in the rebellion against the breadwinner ethic was Hugh Hefner, founder and publisher of *Playboy* magazine. In *The Hearts of Men* she theorizes that the real meaning of Hugh Hefner's work is quite different from a mere pandering to the salacious appetites of American men.

> The real message was not eroticism, but escape— literal escape from the bondage of breadwinning. For that, the breasts and bottoms were necessary not just to sell the magazine, but to protect it. When in the first issue, Hefner talked about staying in his apartment, listening to music and discussing Picasso, there was a Marilyn Monroe centerfold to let you know that there as nothing queer about those indoor pleasures. . . . In every issue, every month, there was a Playmate to prove that a playboy didn't have to be a husband to be a man.[11]

Hugh Hefner (along with the medical establishment, which dramatized stories of overworked men collapsing from stress, and the beat movement, which glorified the nonconforming rebel) thus gave American men permission to opt out of the breadwinner ethic, to spend their money on themselves, cultivating their tastes for the foods, wines, and automobiles that *Playboy*'s advertisers had to offer. In the wake of this male rebellion came a number of sweeping changes in the terms of the American contract—the "sexual revolution," the feminization of poverty, and the revival of feminism.

For men Hefner made fashionable a kind of consumption that previously would have been regarded as effete or even effeminate. But Hefner also had another impact on the culture, which can be strongly linked to the anxieties that so many American women have today about their bodies.

Peep shows and erotic postcards existed long before Hefner was born, and images of women have long had a central role in advertising and popular art. But the pervasiveness of eroticized imagery of women in movies, magazines, and advertising is a post–World War II phenomenon. While the sexualized images of women in advertising, film, and television—more socially sanctioned media—lack the explicitness of *Playboy* centerfolds, the imagery of the magazines has defined the erotic frame of reference from which those less explicit figures draw their symbolism. Today the images of women used to sell everything from Calvin Klein jeans to Budweiser beer present women in erotic postures once only seen in girlie magazines. These images are today so commonplace that we scarcely notice them, but it is important to remember that they are a very recent addition to our cultural landscape.

Where did this appetite for images of women come from? The foldout was the successor to the wartime pinups, the erotic images used by men largely deprived of contact with real women. But the persistent popularity of these images after the war seems puzzling: Back at home at war's end, men were no longer deprived of contact with real women.

Or were they?

Susanne Kappeler sheds some light on this question in her essay "Why Look at Women?", a provocative rereading of John Berger's essay "Why Look at Animals?" in which the British art historian examines how capitalism has transformed the relationship between humans and animals. Until the nineteenth century, Berger argues, "animals were with man at the center of his world. Such centrality was of course economic and productive. Whatever the changes in productive means and social organization, men depended upon animals for food, work, transport, clothing."

As the economic and technological transformation of human society have broken down that intimate bond, the

way humans see—and look at—animals has been transformed. It was precisely when animals became marginal to
human society that our particular interest in looking at them
emerged; thus the emergence of zoos and of the countless
picture books for children about animals, and the rise in
popularity of stuffed animals as toys for children. They all
invite us to heal in fantasy a painful rupture in our reality.

Kappeler extends the analogy to the situation of women:
"Peep shows signal a period where women are disappearing
from daily life, where the category of woman 'has lost its
central importance.'" What Kappeler is saying here isn't literally that women were disappearing from daily life, but
rather that the traditional women's roles of homemaker and
mother were no longer valued by the culture. In the wake of
Hefner's revolt, women returned to the workforce in
increasing numbers, compelled by a combination of economic necessity and a prevailing ideology that denigrated
homemaking and promised fulfillment in careers.

But the increased presence of females in the workplace
only fueled men's nostalgia for the vanished species of
women, Kappeler argues:

> The absorption of individual women into public life
> means the distancing of these women from the cate-
> gory of 'women' and granting them (surrogate)
> human status . . . the existence that counts (ideolog-
> ically, culturally) is not absolute existence, but exis-
> tence which impinges on man, his daily life, his
> consciousness. And from these, animals and women,
> as significant categories, are disappearing fast. They
> reappear as meat on his plate and in his leisure mag-
> azines, in ever-increasing abundance.[12]

Although different societies divided labor along gender
lines in different ways, women always had central and

essential productive roles, not only in the birthing and nurturing of offspring, but also in the great amount of production that occurred within the household: food processing and cooking, and the production of clothing. But changes in the economy and technology meant that women's reproductive capacity was often a liability rather than an asset, and women's household industry was made obsolete by the relentless expansion of industrial production.

Women in the fifties and sixties were, then, at a crisis point. Womanhood, as traditionally understood, had been made obsolete. To justify their continued existence, new work would have to be found for them. They could try doing men's work, of course, at the price of denying their gender identity. Or, as Hefner proposed, they could try to become playmates. (Bob Guccione, founder of *Penthouse* magazine, used the more explicit term "pet.") In effect, the sexual revolution broke the sexual monopoly of marriage among middle-class Americans, creating a free market in sexual goods and services, understood as commodities that women provided to men in exchange for economic security, thereby forcing union shops to compete with lower-cost producers. Rather than give the work to employees whom the employer was obliged to provide with pension plans and other benefits, the buyer could farm out the work on a contract basis. The result, which has parallels throughout the contemporary economy, is massive layoffs in the high-wage labor force, with many workers forced to retrain in mid-career. No surprise that soon, in *The Total Woman*, Marabel Morgan would come along and tell a generation of American wives how Saran Wrap could help them hold on to their man.

The job a generation of women had trained for was rendered obsolete. By the early fifties, women had been pushed out of the workforce and into the kitchen, where there was much less work for them to do than there had been before. Thanks to convenience foods and labor-saving home appliances, men didn't need women to cook for them, and increasingly, it seemed they didn't want their wives to bear children. For a time in the fifties, large families had been in vogue, but by the end of the sixties, the tide was turning. The pill made childbearing a choice.

Ellen Peck, a popular advice columnist of the era, wrote a bestselling book, *The Baby Trap*, with a simple message: Having children is hazardous to your marriage and your personal growth. "Usually, there is a choice to be made. Take your pick. One or the other. Housework and children—or the glamour, involvement and excitement of a free life."[13] Peck continued:

> In the course of writing this book, I've talked to women of many ages, with children and without. The girls I've talked to who don't have children are, almost without exception, prettier, more conversational, more aware, more alive, more exciting, more satisfied. They have, almost without exception, better marriages and happier husbands than those wives who do have children. . . .[14]

What's a wife to do when childbearing is no longer valued, and the meatloaf and mashed potatoes she learned from her mother are now available as TV dinners? Ellen Peck suggested that her readers follow the example of Helen, an East Coast magazine editor who decorated her husband's den to be "comfortable and sexy: there's lots of fake leopard, which David likes. . . . I fix him a drink and settle him down, like a geisha . . . then I serve him dinner." Cooking was still part of the job description, but as Carole Ann, a magazine editor from LA explained:

> Even this has to be an adventure. We both love good food and wine . . . and I have a cabinet filled with

spices, so I experiment. And we'll talk while I'm getting dinner, usually, . . . and finally sit down with the
candlelight reflecting in the wineglasses—yes, that's
every night. There is one thing, you see, that can
never be routine: and that's romance.

To keep romance from becoming routine, Peck recommended *Cosmopolitan* as a good source of "sex-kitten" ideas
for keeping husbands happy. But these ideas apparently
worked only for women who hadn't turned into mothers, "a
change that, if it occurs, makes using sex-kitten ideas difficult, incongruous, perhaps ridiculous."

The emergence of the mass market in objectifying, eroticized images of women, starting in the early fifties, and the
devaluing of women's traditional roles in homemaking and
food preparation is no coincidence. Nor is the emergence of
Julia Child. For a particular group of American women Child
offered a solution to the problem posed by Betty Friedan: a
way to elaborate the self in the domestic environment, a
way to give new meaning to a way of life that was being rendered more and more marginal by the accumulation of
labor-saving devices and convenience foods.

Mastering the Art of French Cooking spoke directly to
those women. Child's cookbook didn't merely promise to
teach women French cooking, it held forth the promise of
mastery: "This is a book for the servantless American cook
who can be unconcerned on occasion with budgets, waistlines, time schedules, children's meals, the parent-den mother
syndrome, or anything else which might interfere with the
enjoyment of producing something wonderful to eat."

It is noteworthy that job pressures and career worries
are not listed among the likely concerns of the intended
audience. Of course, the word "servantless" also had a special resonance for women who often felt like servants. But
Child was not writing for housewives, or at least she was

writing for an audience consisting in large part of women who did not want to think of themselves as housewives. When *From Julia Child's Kitchen* appeared in 1975, Child told John Kifner of the *New York Times* that the book was for "people whose hobby is food, not for housewives." Kifner explained: "The word 'housewives,' in her vocabulary, ranks with 'home economists' as a term to be disdained.[15]

Just as motivational researcher Ernst Dichter advised cake-mix manufacturers to reformulate their products to require the cook to add an egg, in order to give their customers the feeling that they were really baking, Julia Child's recipes were formulated to require many ingredients and many steps—and often most of the available cookware. "The Frenchman takes his greatest pleasure from a well-known dish impeccably cooked and served," Child informed her readers. "A perfect navarin of lamb, for instance, requires a number of operations including brownings, simmerings, strainings, skimmings and flavorings. Each of the several steps in the process, though simple to accomplish, plays a critical role, and if any is eliminated or combined with another, the texture and taste of the navarin suffer."[16]

Not all Frenchmen or other serious gourmets were impressed with this approach to haute cuisine. In *The Taste of America,* published in 1977, John and Karen Hess dissect, skewer, and lambast(e) Child at considerable length as a pretentious gastronomic poseur. After citing several cases of recipes that don't work well or are inauthentic, they approvingly cite the comment of French gastronome Robert Courtine about a crepe recipe that appeared in a Time-Life book edited by M. F. K. Fisher, Michael Field, and Child. The recipe, which calls for thirty-three ingredients in five separate steps, is "a lot of work for such a meager result!" Courtine remarked. "It's the sort of dish to dazzle and beguile a foreign woman but it is false grand cuisine and as ungastronomic as can be."[17]

If Child helped to resolve a crisis in the lives of middle-class American women, she also helped to resolve a crisis in the American economy, whose ever-growing productive capacity was stymied by a set of social values that had been carried over from the Great Depression and the war years. These values emphasized production and savings over consumption, and social solidarity and equality over class consciousness.

Motivational researcher Ernst Dichter, a consultant to major manufacturing companies, described the dilemma of the American economy as follows:

> We are now confronted with the problem of permitting the average American to feel moral . . . even when he is spending, even when he is not saving, even when he is taking two vacations a year and buying a second or third car. One of the basic problems of prosperity, then, is to demonstrate that the hedonistic approach to life is a moral, not an immoral one.[18]

If Julia Child had not existed, the American economy would have had to invent her. The creation of a consumer society required more than the development of new products; it also required overcoming a pervasive ethic of frugality. During World War II, Allied propaganda stressed the equality of all Americans and the nobility of the ordinary citizen, who sacrificed for the common good. Lavish consumption was selfish, unpatriotic, and unfair to all the others, who were making do without. Who better to break down the barriers against conspicuous consumption than an old-time Yankee? Who could give permission to consume escargots and blanquette de veau with more authority than this living embodiment of traditional American values?

Just as Hugh Hefner gave a generation of American men permission to stop being breadwinners, Julia Child gave a broad section of the emerging managerial class permission to opt out of the social contract.

We haven't yet come to grips with the meaning of this foodie revolution. In the early years the story of the foodie revolution was told as a story of human liberation, a passage from bondage into freedom or from darkness into light. In the bad old days, so this story goes, we ate canned vegetables and meatloaf. Food was merely fuel, until we rose up, threw off the shackles of culinary puritanism, and for the first time discovered the pleasures of the palate.

At first blush the enthusiasm that greeted the foodie revolution sounds a lot like the enthusiasm with which America embraced the sexual revolution. At just about the same time that the missionary position gave way to a whole catalog of polymorphously perverse pleasures, Americans discovered the vast potential for pleasure right at the tip of their tongues. An oppressive regime had been overthrown, opening up new vistas, not merely for pleasure, but for human self-realization. "Cooking has entered a grand era of liberation," proclaimed James Beard in 1980.[19]

Writing in 1986, cookbook author Irena Chalmers, one of the new celebrities created by the foodie revolution, was a bit more cautious in her enthusiasm than James Beard had been, but no less sweeping. She described the changes taking place on the American food scene as part of

> a social revolution that is making astonishing, radical changes in how we live now, and how we live in the future. We will be as altered as the French after the fall of Louis XVI, as the Russians after the abdication of the Czar. The difference is that this revolution is benign. At the moment, we are hardly feeling a thing. But that is also what they said about the guillotine.[20]

The comparison to the French and Russian revolutions may seem absurd; how can one compare the proliferation of cooking classes and expensive restaurants and an increase in quiche and crepe consumption to a series of events as dramatic and transformative as the overthrow of the French monarchy or the "ten days that shook the world"?

The answer may be that whereas the French Revolution proclaimed the ideals of liberty, equality, and fraternity, and marked the beginning of a historical epoch marked by the rise of democratic ideal and the leveling of class distinctions, the foodie revolution, in its own modest way, can be seen as a marker for the end of that era. In its wake have come the decline of the civic culture and the rise of the consumer culture.

While the French and Russian revolutions were uprisings of the oppressed masses against a tyrannical ruling class, the foodie revolution was an uprising by the middle and upper classes, what the late social historian Christopher Lasch termed a "revolt of the elites."

"The general course of recent history no longer favors the leveling of social distinctions but runs more and more in the direction of a two-class society in which the favored few monopolize the advantages of money, education and power," Lasch observed in *The Revolt of the Elites*.[21] In our time "the democraticization of abundance—the expectation that each generation would enjoy a standard of living beyond the reach of its predecessors—has given way to a reversal in which age-old inequalities are beginning to reestablish themselves, sometimes at a frightening rate, sometimes so gradually as to escape notice."

The reestablishment of the "age-old inequalities" would not have been possible without the moral transformation that Ernst Dichter had called for in the early fifties. By the early 80s, it was in full swing, formally inaugurated at Ronald Reagan's first inaugural ball. Writing in 1985, playwright and actor Wallace Shawn captured the spirit of the new moral order:

> More and more people who grew up around me are making this decision; they are throwing away their moral chains and learning to enjoy their true situation: Yes, they are admitting loudly and bravely, we live in beautiful homes, we're surrounded by beautiful gardens, our children are playing with wonderful toys, and our kitchen shelves are filled with wonderful food.
>
> The amazing thing I've noticed about those friends of mine who've made that choice is that as soon as they've made it, they begin to blossom, to flower. . . . They can enjoy a bottle of wine or a walk in the garden with unmixed pleasure, because they feel justified in having the bottle of wine, in having the garden.[22]

This revolt of the elites depended, fundamentally, on a group of Americans coming to recognize themselves as having a distinct identity—a set of tastes and habits that set them apart—and then finding sanction to opt out of the social contract that sustained the democratic, egalitarian ideal. This is, at its heart, what the foodie revolution is all about.

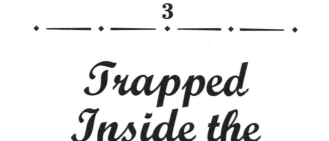

3

Trapped Inside the Magic Kingdom

More and more, we appear to be a nation of overfed clowns living in a hostile cartoon environment.
—James Howard Kunstler,
The Geography of Nowhere:
The Rise and Decline of America's Man-Made Landscape

It's impossible to make sense of the disordered American way of eating without looking at what's happening to the rest of the American way of life.

In a *Time* magazine essay that seeks to capture the zeitgeist of the nineties, Robert Wright laments:

Whether burdened by an overwhelming flurry of daily commitments or stifled by a sense of social isolation (or oddly, both), whether mired for hours in a sense of life's pointlessness or beset for days by unresolved anxiety; whether deprived by long workweeks from quality time with offspring or drowning in quantity time with them—whatever the source of stress, we at times get the feeling that modern life isn't what we were designed for.[1]

But the trouble we have with food isn't simply the consequence of responding to living in anxious times by eating compulsively; rather, it's that we are caught in an existential double whammy. Everything that has gone wrong with the American way of life is replicated in the American way of eating: a sense that reality is slipping away from us, an anxious feeling that things are falling apart, a fear of lurking but invisible dangers.

There are at least three different aspects to this sense that reality is slipping away, and each has its parallel in our relationship to food.

First, there is the deterioration or disintegration of many of the long-standing institutions around which Americans have built their lives. The old neighborhood is a slum, and the new neighborhood isn't a neighborhood. It isn't safe to let the kids go to the park by themselves, the American League has a designated-hitter rule, and who knows whether Social Security will be around when we are ready to retire.

Second, we are becoming increasingly aware that we live in a socially constructed reality, and that all the official versions of reality in which we once put our faith—versions set forth by churches, political leaders, or the news media—are just stories. With this realization has come a great uncertainty about values, and for some, a hunger for absolutes.

And third, the everyday reality in which people used to live their lives has been steadily replaced by a virtual reality (or hyperreality, as some have called it). It has become customary to use the term "virtual reality" to refer to the interactive world of the Internet or to interactive computer games, but the term applies equally well to a world constructed of images and symbols—the world we immerse ourselves in when we watch television, go to movies, or spend our working days staring at a computer screen or a spreadsheet, looking at characters and figures that are representations of some other reality. And it also applies to the mall, the theme park, the theme restaurant, and other controlled environments that purvey packaged experiences.

Each of these erosions of reality has its counterpart in our relationship to food:

The stable food institutions of earlier times included the idea of regular mealtimes, a limited diet of foods dictated by season and tradition, and the custom of the family meal. In its push to create new markets, the food industry has invested immense resources in creating entire new categories of foods designed for between-meal snacking, and untold billions of dollars on selling us the idea. The limited diet of foods dictated by season and tradition has also fallen by the wayside, as global trade and a multicultural society have broadened our horizons. And the custom of the family meal has largely vanished in most households, a victim of hectic lifestyles and conflicting schedules.

The sense of certainty about what to eat has also deteriorated. Most of us were brought up in an era when the gospel of the four food groups ruled supreme, and there was little of the current concern about cholesterol and fat. The foods depicted as symbolizing a healthy diet in the classroom nutrition charts of our childhoods—big slabs of red meat, chunks of cheese, and bottles of whole milk—have been recast under the new dispensation as silent killers.

And real food is increasingly being replaced by virtual food, in either of two senses. On the one hand, there is a large category of foods—and eating experiences—in which the image of the product becomes inseparable from the experience of eating it. This is particularly true of brand-name foods. And on the other hand, there are the technologically engineered "fake foods," which are simulations of something they are not: butter substitutes that contain no fat, lemonade that contains no lemon juice, mayonnaise that contains no eggs, beers and wines that contain no alcohol.

If you think of yourself as a red-blooded American, the mere mention of the word *postmodern* makes you wish you had a gun. But the fact of the matter is that if you *are* a red-blooded American, you probably *are* consuming a post-modern diet: a pastiche of granola and Twinkies, Hunan chicken and *penne arrabbiata*, Big Macs and Häagen-Dazs that staggers drunkenly across the boundaries of culture, class, and history.

The result is gastrovertigo, a peculiarly postmodern kind of indigestion, characterized by an increasing inability to tell reality from fantasy, with your stomach caught in the middle. And don't try to adjust your mind-set, because it isn't just you. It really *is* getting harder to tell reality and fantasy apart.

JIMINY CRICKET TRIED TO WARN US

Long before the first McDonald's ever hoisted its Golden Arches, long before the first Weight Watchers weigh-in, and long before any American had ever heard of sun-dried toma-toes or radicchio, we were warned. Our current troubles with food were foreshadowed with prophetic insight in Walt Disney's 1940 retelling of Carlo Collodi's children's classic, *Pinocchio*.

Pinocchio's Pleasure Island wasn't quite so well stocked with goodies as the modern supermarket, but fifty years ago, lobster blini, microwave chimichangas, and Screaming Yellow Zonkers were simply beyond the imagination of even Disney's staff of fantasists. Pinocchio's orgy of gastronomic self-indulgence seems rather tame compared to the fantasies our glossy food magazines can conjure up, but it still isn't hard to get the point of Disney's little morality tale.

Pinocchio, as you may recall, was on his way to school, and on his way to becoming a real human being (a goal to be achieved by diligence, hard work, and delayed gratifications), when he was lured away by the promises of easy pleasures to Pleasure Island, a hedonistic paradise where little boys could eat and ransack to their hearts' content. Jiminy Cricket, his faithful conscience, pleaded with him not to succumb to temptation, but Pinocchio would not listen.

It was only in the nick of time, after he had begun to sprout donkey ears and lose the power of speech, that Pinocchio recognized a sinister reality lurking beneath the glittering surfaces. The little boys, once their transformation into donkeys was complete, were shipped off to the salt mines to spend the rest of their lives as beasts of burden.

As a culture we are reaching that same stage of disenchantment with the Magic Kingdom. When we first discovered Pleasure Island—and Cuisinarts and Dijon mustard—it felt like liberation: freedom from the old taboos, freedom to explore a new world of pleasures. But the illusion no longer holds us in its thrall, and we are starting to sense the loss of our humanity. We have had as much fun as we can stand, and we want to go home now, please.

Pinocchio was able to flee Pleasure Island and escape back to the real world. But for us it isn't likely to be quite as easy. For starters the real world isn't what it used to be, and besides, Walt Disney isn't on our side anymore. The animator's legacy is a global empire of Pleasure Islands.

THE SMASHING OF THE CERTAINTIES

Whereas middle-class Americans could once anticipate a career that would last a lifetime, few jobs in today's labor market offer that kind of security. Job changes are more likely to resemble desperate leaps from one ice floe to the next than a steady climb up a corporate ladder.

And each change in employment comes at a cost to the self, as the anxious applicant must refashion his or her résumé and persona to fit into a new situation. "The smashing of the certainties on which we used to build our lives goes on and on and on," lamented Gerald Meyer, after being fired for the third time from a position as a former McDonnell Douglas Corp. executive.[2]

Meyer is part of what Secretary of Labor Robert Reich has termed the anxious class, the millions of middle-class Americans whose visions of the American dream have collided with a set of social and economic realities that have caught them unprepared.

The anxiety that so many Americans feel isn't really about food so much as it is about our futures—and our identities. But food plays a central role in the way many of us cope with those anxieties, and food marketing increasingly promises us that we can recapture a sense of wholeness by eating "real beef, real food," or even Arby's real chicken.

As Gerard Harrington, managing editor of Trends Research Institute's quarterly *Trends Journal*, explains: "There is a growing sense of depression in the country due to the fact that this industrial age is ending and people are losing faith in the systems and institutions that are supposed to enrich their lives."[3] To combat consumers' lack of trust in institutions, "marketers will be offering comfort and hope [in 1995] . . . using various key words like 'genuine' and 'trust' to nurture consumers—a trend that's likely to continue next year."[4]

Take, for example, an advertisement seen on the marquee outside an Arby's restaurant:

CHICKEN FINGERS
REAL CHICKEN
REAL TASTE

You don't need to be a semiotician to interpret the layers of meaning in this simple three-line message, but it helps to have a working knowledge of American fast-food history.

"Chicken Fingers" is Arby's trademarked name for its brand of skinless, boneless breaded chicken strips. "Real chicken" alludes subtly to the fact that rival McDonald's Chicken McNuggets are made from chopped chicken meat. (In their original formulation they also contained chicken skin.) As for "real taste," this claim addresses one of the most commonly voiced consumer complaints about factory chickens—that they are flavorless.

Introduced in 1984, Chicken McNuggets were a technological and marketing breakthrough—a new fast-food product that capitalized on the growing consumer demand for chicken and yet was more convenient than fried chicken, a market segment dominated by fast-food competitor KFC. McNuggets could more easily be eaten without utensils—for example, while driving.

Chicken McNuggets were an overnight sensation, creating a major new market segment for McDonald's. Competitors raced to develop their own versions, and compensated for their late entry into the market by offering products made from whole pieces of chicken—"real chicken."

Of course, the commercial "real chicken" is essentially a factory product, genetically engineered to reach slaughter weight in a mere seven weeks, fed a diet that includes subclinical doses of antibiotics as a growth stimulant, raised indoors in an environment whose rhythms are electronically controlled and monitored, and slaughtered on an assembly line by human workers who mimic the routines of robots.

But Arby's chicken is real at least in the sense that it is not pressed and formed from chopped chicken parts. There is an irony to Arby's making this claim for their chicken, since Arby's empire was built on a processed, pressed, and formed roast beef product whose ontological status is roughly equivalent to that of a Chicken McNugget—that is, it's made from chopped, pressed beef parts.

What is happening to our food is also happening to us.

We live, work and die in increasingly managed environments. We are assessed, graded, sorted, and culled by scientific management methods. It may be difficult for the modern office worker to muster much sympathy for the calf or chicken condemned to spend its entire life in a cubicle, exposed only to artificial light, deprived of social contact, when his or her own life is becoming increasingly similar. The strategies used to stimulate our appetites and manage our behaviors are a little more complex than those used in animal husbandry, but the idea is basically the same.

As benign as it sounds, the Arby's slogan cleverly addresses an underlying feeling that haunts many Americans: a growing sense of unreality that manifests itself in a wide variety of ways: in the increased prevalence of anxiety disorders, in the growing popularity of conspiracy theories, and in a growing nostalgia for a time before everything got so complicated.

"Real" has become one of the buzzwords of the food world. The "real" symbol has become a service mark for the dairy industry, the beef industry touts "real beef, real food," and frozen pizzas boast that they are made with real cheese.

Marketers have embedded a prelapsarian vision in many food products: Eden Farms, Nature's Valley, Country Time, and Country Blend, to name a few. And the more estranged from the natural the product is, the more essential it is that the product be packaged and marketed as natural. Country Time lemonade, in its original formulation, contained no lemon juice but was aggressively marketed with the imagery of a bygone pastorale: grandpa playing checkers in the country store. Put all these images together and what emerges is a picture of the world we have lost: It may never have existed, but its hold on the public imagination is as powerful as the image of Eden.

We live in a time when there is a great hunger for the real. "Real" offers reassurance to consumers trapped in a world of artifice. If you live in Rock Creek Estates, but there are no rocks, no creeks, and no estates there, and if it doesn't feel like a real neighborhood, and if your doctor has suggested that you switch from butter to something that looks and tastes like butter, then there is something reassuring about the promise of real chicken. There is in unspoken suggestion that this product offers a gateway to the lost world, a more natural state of being. In the supermarket the hunger for the real and the hunger for the lost world come together.

There was a time when the artifice of food scientists was seen as tangible evidence of human progress, when each new product, from Miracle Whip to Jell-O to Carnation Instant Breakfast, was embraced as a victory against death itself. "The day is coming," one writer exulted, "when a woman can buy a boiled dinner and carry it home in her purse . . . when a well-stocked pantry will be reduced to a few boxes . . . when you'll serve the girls a bridge luncheon of dehydrated meat and potatoes with powdered potatoes and powdered onions, a dehydrated cabbage salad, and custard made with powdered eggs and powdered milk for dessert."[5]

The most powerful attraction of these new processed foods was never their convenience, and certainly not their flavor. Rather, they were tokens of modernity, sacraments of a faith in a way of life in which science and reason prevailed over custom and superstition. The natural world was there for us to conquer and remold. This was the American dream, for which generations of Americans gladly forsook their old identities and foodways.

Somehow the dream went sour. The same instant mashed potatoes and nondairy creamer that had been symbols of progress in the fifties within a very short time became symbols of something vastly different. What took place wasn't simply a change in tastes but the collapse of a vision: a loss of faith in the American dream. And with it came a nostalgia for the real, a hunger for an America that no longer exists.

THE HOSTILE CARTOON ENVIRONMENT

Today our politics and our foodstuffs crisscross the boundaries between reality and representation, leaving the line hopelessly blurred. Politicians appear in public to create photo opportunities for transmission through the image world. It is useless to wonder what they are "really like," since what they are really like—assuming that they are really like anything—is irrelevant. What matters is their image.

As with reality, so with food. Increasingly our diet is filled with simulacra, products that are designed to look and taste like real apples, real beer, real butter and cheese, real soft drinks, and so on. And yet they are not real. Of some we must either say that they are not real foods, because they do not nourish, or else change our definition of food. They are designed to enable us to simulate the sensations of eating without actually achieving satiety. And we stand at the threshold of a great leap forward in the world of simulated eating: New nondigestible fat substitutes, such as Olestra and Simplesse, will give rise to a new varieties of ice cream and potato chips that can be eaten without the risk of weight gain.

Is that strawberry in the supermarket produce section a real strawberry, or is it only a genetically engineered representation of a strawberry, perfect in shape and color, but lacking flavor? "It's not nice to fool Mother Nature," insisted a memorable television commercial for a margarine that is supposed to taste like butter. But the artificial flavors have become so ubiquitous that in some taste tests, consumers have preferred them to the genuine article.

THE WORLD WE HAVE LOST

We are a nation of immigrants. When our ancestors came to these shores, two or five or ten generations ago, they brought with them patterns of eating rooted in the history, culture, and agriculture of their homelands. Few of these traditions survived long in the new world. The new immigrants were eager to shed the habits that marked them as foreigners, and quickly seized the trappings of the American way of life.

The traditional family meal has all but disappeared. Meals were a centerpoint of family life, an organized daily ritual that reaffirmed for every member the fact that being a part of a family was a core element of his or her identity. Gone with it is the security that regular routines bring to life, the daily symbolism of nurturance.

For better and for worse, the simple interactions of the meal carried with them important affirmations of the role and identity of every member of the family. Even if getting Junior and Sis to wash and dry the dishes was often more trouble than it was worth, important lessons were conveyed. Junior might have whined a little when he was told to stop playing and come indoors and wash his hands because it was time to eat, but the underlying message was a positive one: We need you here; we don't want to start without you. Stories were told—not only about the hard day at the office or on the shop floor, but also the family lore, accumulated over generations.

There is no need to feel overly nostalgic about the family meal of the fifties, though. Mealtime was also an important time for transmitting patriarchal gender roles. Father was the head of the household, and in working-class families it was customary that he would be served first, and would receive the largest portion. Mother's performance in the subservient roles of cook and waitress, if done well, was rewarded with praise and compliments. And yet, if these roles were constricting or oppressive, especially for women, they also gave definition and order. And even if we are well rid of the rituals of patriarchy, we have yet to evolve suitable replacements.

Rather, the ritual of the family meal has largely been replaced by an irregular pattern that differs for each member of the family. Breakfast is eaten on the run, lunch is often fast food, and attendance at the family dinner table is so unpredictable that the effort that would be required to prepare a common meal is hardly warranted—assuming that anyone in the family knows how and has time.

The decline of the family meal may be bad news for Western civilization, but it's good news for credit card companies. "Gone are the days when Dad came home at six o'clock, dinner was ready on the table, and the entire family enjoyed a meal and the evening together," declares a news release reporting the findings of the 1995 *MasterCard Dining Out Study*:

> In the 1990s, more families have dual incomes, children are more independent, and 25 percent of Americans work at home or have a home office. Combine this with more than 100 channels on television, personal computers and video games, and it's not surprising that today's families are too distracted in their own homes to spend quality time with each other."[6]

Happily, the study reports, harried families can spend quality time at restaurants.

The increasingly common patterns are snacking and "grazing." Americans spend tens of billions annually on snack foods, and the food industry spends hundreds of millions advertising them. One important significance of this shift is that eating—traditionally a fundamentally social activity—is today increasingly a private one.

What we eat has also changed. Back in the era when America was still a predominantly agricultural society, most of the foods Americans ate were produced and consumed locally. Potatoes and root crops were stored in the root cellar, and vegetables from the garden were canned. Cabbage was made into sauerkraut, and cucumbers into pickles. Only farm families made their own sausages or cured their own hams, of course, but even for those who didn't, much of the daily diet was locally produced: meat and sausage from the local butcher, canned vegetables from the local cannery, which bought from the local farmer.

Although immigrants brought with them food traditions as diverse as their ethnic heritages, most eventually abandoned those traditions in favor of a more modern American diet, eating the foods that they saw advertised in magazines and newspapers.

Convenience foods had already begun to make their appearance as early as the thirties, but the extent of processing continued to expand over the decades.

The shift to an increasingly processed diet has a variety of implications. Those relating to health are most frequently discussed: In practice, food processing very often means adding fat or sugar and removing fiber. When broilers are turned into fried chicken, or potatoes into potato chips, or wheat into bread, the calorie content is increased and the density of other nutrients reduced.

But another less noticed implication of the shift to a processed diet is the increased consumption of symbols. Virtually everything we consume nowadays comes in a package, and every package carries a message, even if only by omission, as in the case of the yellow-and-black generic packaging. A world of irregular natural forms is replaced by a preinterpreted world of packages. The reality, when you get home, when you unpack the frozen cartons of microwavable Budget Gourmet chicken tetrazzini and the Wolfgang Puck pizza, is that the products never taste quite as good as they look on the package. The reality never quite lives up to the fantasy.

REALITY ISN'T WHAT IT USED TO BE

We pass through time as though on a train. The landscape changes so gradually that we barely notice, but over time, it changes so much that the world we knew when we boarded has virtually disappeared, and the world that we see from our window seems strange and new. The great transformation that we see is the ongoing gradual replacement of the natural world by a manufactured one—endless stretches of the countryside transformed into subdivisions, endlessly repeating highway images of golden arches and the logo of the old Kentucky gentleman with the white beard.

The way the postmodern story is usually told, human history is a progression from traditional to modern to postmodern. In traditional societies what we ate and what we worshiped and how we parsed reality were all well-established matters of tradition, stable over generations.

As the pace of change accelerated, new inventions overthrew old beliefs, and the old order based on religion was overthrown by a new order based on science and invention, wedded to a faith in progress and human rationality. In a frenzy of invention, every element of the old ways of eating was overthrown. Science overcame superstition as Europeans were persuaded to eat tomatoes and potatoes. And then, in the last few decades, shaken by the horrors of two world wars and the possibility of nuclear holocaust, we have seen the steady erosion of this centuries-old faith in reason and progress.

In this sense we can be said to be living in a postmodern food world. We entered the modern era during the first half of this century, as waves of American immigrants were persuaded to forsake their traditional ways of eating in favor of a new diet, grounded in the principle of scientific nutrition, that marked them as Americans. Every child learned the gospel of the four food groups, devised by the U.S. Department of Agriculture and promoted by the National Dairy

Council. The collapse of this modern order of eating started in the sixties—and with it, a decline of faith in science and progress and that body of values and beliefs known as Americanism.

Modernity stripped away all the frameworks of tradition but never provided an adequate replacement. It made promises that it couldn't keep, and increasingly it came up against the limits of the natural world. One problem was simply a widening reality gap. Consumers were faithfully purchasing, preparing, and consuming the foods that the nutrionists prescribed, but they weren't "building strong bodies twelve ways," as the Wonder Bread ads promised. Rather, the incidence of cancer and heart disease increased, and a growing chorus of voices began to question the healthfulness of the high-protein, red-meat-and-egg diet recommended by the nutrition establishment.

THE SOCIAL CONSTRUCTION OF REALITY

Our loss of faith in the nutrition experts is only a small part of a larger pattern. Today many Americans have little belief in the credibility of the news media or the truthfulness of their elected officials. The core doctrines of their religious traditions, held with unquestioning faith by countless previous generations, are likewise increasingly questioned or else simply dismissed.

There is a growing sense that the stories we tell ourselves about our past, our present, and ourselves are just that—constructions, stories. In place of a belief in absolute truth or objectivity, many Americans are coming to believe that our way of seeing the world is only one among many. Any hope that we once had of establishing the right way of seeing the world is rapidly fading, and with it, our firm grasp on the nature of reality. We have learned instead to be pragmatic in choosing between different constructions of reality: whether to proceed on the premise that it is our electrolytes or our yin and yang that are out of balance may ultimately be decided on the basis of which kind of medicine our insurance plan will pay for.

Since time immemorial (that is, before we started telling these stories), the making of these stories—creation myths, folk tales, psychoanalytic theories—has been a central human enterprise. What has changed is that the manufacture and dissemination of these stories has become a much more self-conscious and organized activity.

Collectively this activity has come to be known as the consciousness industry—the vast panoply of publishers, studio executives, journalists, producers, directors, copywriters, advertisers, cinematographers, video producers, models, animation specialists, market researchers, and so on who produce an endless outpouring of television programs, films, commercials, press releases, magazine articles, advertisements, and so on and on and on. And, perhaps most important, the sum total of these stories has increasingly come to coalesce into a picture so complete in its scope that we can think of it as another reality—even a higher reality.

LIVING THE VIRTUAL LIFE

Is it live, or is it Memorex? Set aside, for the moment, all those contentious arguments about the social construction of reality. Even if you don't buy into the postmodern notion that the basic categories within which we perceive the world are socially constructed, it seems hard to deny that the lived experience of Americans in the late twentieth century is a manufactured product. The average adult spends twenty-eight hours a week watching a televised version of reality, and countless additional hours per week taking in the representations of reality conveyed by radio, video, and print. For many middle-class Americans, add in the hours of our working day that we spend looking at screens or pages filled with columns of figures or executive summaries that purport to be representations of some aspect of reality. As production gets rationalized, even the real—for example, the student in the classroom, the patient in the hospital—becomes a set of data to be processed. Increasingly, through all these media, we spend our waking hours immersed in a world of symbols, representations of a reality beyond our immediate aquaintance.

TELEVISION CONSTRUCTS OUR COMMON REALITY

The foundation of any social reality is a body of common knowledge. In a traditional community in which mass media are primitive or nonexistent, the body of common knowledge is created and circulated by face-to-face contact. Even within that kind of community, though, it is possible to speak of different degrees of reality: The events that happen in public spaces or that become common knowledge are in some sense more real than the events that happen in private space. By extension, in the post-television world, the most real events, in the sense of being the most widely shared, are the ones that are experienced via the mass media. In some ways the world that television projects before us is more real than the world of our own "unmediated" experience. Even our most intimate interpersonal experiences are increasingly mediated by the symbols and values of the advertised reality, and the set of meanings that television conveys is more coherent and universal than the meanings of our unmediated experiences.

Television is the place where things happen in our lives that we can talk about with our neighbors. Of course, we don't really know our neighbors very well; not nearly as well as we used to before television came into our lives, and not as well as we know Seinfeld and Roseanne and David Letterman. And our ability to talk to the neighbors about what we saw on television also seems to be decreasing; unlike the days when everyone watched *Bonanza* and the *Dick Van Dyke Show*, today each of us can choose a more private reality by surfing the cable channels.

The world manufactured by the consciousness industries is no longer separable from the "real" one. Back in the 1950s, when Daniel Boorstin created the term "pseudo-event" to describe events that were staged for the benefit of the news media, it was still possible to imagine a meaningful distinction between a "real" world and an imaginary world created by the media. Today television and the movies don't simply construct for us a picture of the world; they give us the vocabulary with which we communicate with each other. Every gesture—whether we eat at McDonald's or Wendy's, arrive at the party with a bottle of Italian Swiss Colony, Kendall-Jackson, or Opus One—has meaning, and it is the world of advertising that defines those meanings. And insofar as it is through those gestures that we proclaim our identity, it is in the power of those advertisers to define that identity.

Television doesn't reflect our reality; rather, it completes it and depletes it. Every channel is a nostalgia channel; if you want to see the neighbors getting together for a good old-fashioned Fourth of July picnic, or the sturdy farm wife wiping her hands on her apron as her kids run off to play on the country road, or if you want to see the inner-city kids, black and white, playing together, it's all there waiting for you on television, if nowhere else.

Every shared reality may be socially constructed, but there are some important differences between living in a reality constructed the old-fashioned way and living in the Magic Kingdom. One difference is simply the rate of change. In the old world, the reputation of a beer, a cheese, or a political leader was something established over years; today these consumer products are known by their images, constructed by the exchange of cash for air time and advertising space. When the cash stops flowing, their images disappear from the screen.

ENTERING GASTRONOMIC HYPERREALITY

It's customary to equate the real with the natural, but both terms of the equation have become increasingly problematic. We understand each term by opposition to something else—the unreal, or the unnatural. There was a time when we could understand the real by contrasting it with events that happened only in a novel, or in the movies, or in our own imaginations. But as we have come increasingly to the view that reality is socially constructed, this understanding has been undermined. Events seen on television by millions are more deeply embedded in our collective consciousness than the events we witness in the "real" world.

The category of the natural also becomes increasingly vacuous. If there is any content to it, it means this: the portion of the physical world that is beyond our manipulation. But that physical world, as Bill McKibben warns in *The End of Nature*, has largely vanished.[7] We live increasingly in a manufactured world, in which the particularity of natural forms gives way to a landscape whose shapes are endlessly reduplicated, and are not only shapes but symbols.

Nowhere is this more true than in the supermarket. It is no accident that the produce section is the first section of the supermarket that you enter. It stands as a shrine to the natural world, a little Garden of Eden, evoking images of the farm. But this is really a Disney replacement of nature: The perfect color of the oranges, the perfect shape of the apples, the grading standards that assure that only unblemished produce can be sold—all contrive to create a fantasy of the natural world.

In the rest of the supermarket, what you see is for the most part not food but packages. The packages speak to the consumer in ways that piles of onions or mounds of lettuce cannot. Sometimes the packages are decorated with pictures of food, often photographed to look more sensuous, more perfect, more inviting than the contents of the package will ever look in real life. Beads of glycerine applied by the food stylist make the plate of turkey tetrazzini "come to life"—glow with an erotic radiance. But not all packages sell sensuality; others connect to our nostalgia, our cravings for security, our desire for status.

Cold cereals are an American invention, and they developed simultaneously with the rise of the American advertising industry. Manufacturers start from whole grains and then add sugar and air. But the most important ingredient they add is symbolism. Often you can buy the same product without the symbolism, on a bottom shelf in a plastic bag for half the price, but few consumers do; the magic is missing. Without the symbolism we have come to attach to the product, it just doesn't taste the same.

THE MAGIC KINGDOM IS EVERYWHERE

No one has done more to blur the distinctions between fantasy and reality than Walt Disney. The mere inconvenience of his death has hardly slowed down Uncle Walt in his wizardry. Widely circulated stories at the time of his death alleged that the father of Mickey and Donald had arranged to be preserved in a state of cryogenic suspended animation. But even if true, this form of immortality has proved superfluous; disembodied, the Disney spirit continues to work his magic on American culture.

Disney's first step across the reality-fantasy barrier was the opening of Disneyland, where children could come and see the characters they had only known in movies or the pages of comic books actually come to life, strolling through Fantasyland and posing for pictures with the kiddies. Disneyland wasn't simply an amusement park but an alternative reality, where dreams really could come true. In addition to all the real people dressed up as Goofys and Mickeys, Walt also populated his park with animatronic robots dressed up as George Washington and Abraham Lincoln, endlessly declaring independence or reciting the Emancipation Proclamation.

At the Les Chefs de France restaurant in EPCOT, three real French chefs have lent their names to a restaurant that serves a Disney interpretation of French cuisine—stereotypical dishes stripped of anything that might give offense. "It's disgusting," confides a real French waiter, "but what can one do?" The customers' vision of France was brought to them by Disney; this is the French food they expect.

The goal, of course, is to deliver not simply food but a fantasy dining experience. The performances of the waiters and waitresses, the Goofys and Mickeys, are as scripted as the performances of the animatronic presidents.

Which is fine, since this is, after all, a fantasy world. The trouble is that this fantasy world has metastasized. As cookie-cutter chain restaurants spread across the land, replicating themselves endlessly in interchangable suburban malls, they too offer packaged, commodified dining experiences.

And yet, for the customer, something is missing. After a long day at Walt Disney World, when you're tired and want to go home, you want to go back into the real world and talk to real people, you walk into McDonald's, where Ronald McDonald waves at you and the kid behind the counter asks you animatronically, "May I take your order?" Is he real, or have you still not escaped the fantasy? Food fun may have started with Disney, but now it is everywhere.

PLEASURE ISLAND AT THE MALL

Today's Pleasure Island is the mall, where all your shopping and eating fantasies come true. It isn't all free, of course, but you can put it on plastic. You can delay payment, but you don't have to delay gratification.

The largest collection of these fantasies under one roof is at the Mall of America, a 4.2-million-square-foot megamall geographically located in a suburb of Minneapolis–St. Paul, but spiritually located everywhere and nowhere. The endless parade of fast-food eateries and theme restaurants on East Broadway or West Market bear little resemblance to any Broadway or Market Street in the world outside, but are virtually indistinguishable from the malls of suburban Houston, Miami, or St. Louis. Many well-known chain eateries are represented, including Ruby Tuesday's, Tony Roma's, Manchu Wok, and Hooters, but you don't have to leave your favorite department store to grab a bite to eat. Bloomingdale's, Sears, and Nordstrom's all have their own in-house restaurants, as does anchor tenant Macy's, where celebrity chef Wolfgang Puck sells designer pizzas. You can also combine eating and shopping at Boogie's Diner, a retro diner and clothing store that offers shakes, malts, fifteen-dollar T-shirts, and five-thousand-dollar leather jackets. If you have the kids in tow, there's Knott's Camp Snoopy, an outpost of Knott's Berry Farm, which offers rides, shops, and Mrs. Knott's fried chicken.

But if you hate that mall atmosphere, you can escape to warm and rustic Tucci Bennuch, a creation of Chicago-based Lettuce Entertain You Inc., known for its high-concept theme restaurants. Steve Ottman, an Entertain You partner, described the concept: "Tuccia and Bennuch are sisters who love cooking and decide they may as well open an eating place." Actually they have opened quite a few, in Chicago, Phoenix, Beverly Hills and elsewhere. "We strive to make our places the farthest thing from being in a mall possible," Ottman told a newspaper reporter.

There may not be much difference between the burgers at Boogie's diner, the Rainforest Cafe, or Planet Hollywood, but each purveys a different fantasy: Boogie's offers a nostalgic trip back into the happy days of the 1950s, the Rainforest Cafe manufactures ersatz adventure in an ambience of plastic foliage and mechanical macaws, and Planet Hollywood indulges the fantasy that you have been admitted past the velvet cord into Arnold Schwarzenegger, Bruce Willis, and Demi Moore's own private club.

The secret to all of these fantasy dining concepts is that each of them sells back a little piece of the world that you have lost, or yearn for. Do you yearn for the wide-open spaces? Try Stuart Anderson's Cattle Company. Do you feel disconnected from the good earth? Dine at the Good Earth. Long for the small-town life you never knew? Try the Cracker Barrel.

Of course, if the fantasy were really convincing, that might be terrifying. But it never is. No matter how many times you go to Planet Hollywood, you never seem to run into Bruce or Demi, and when you really stop to think about it, the very concept of an authentic Italian trattoria in a suburban mall doesn't even make sense.

The restaurant dining experience is in greater or lesser degree a marketing experience. Every element of our interaction with the establishment, from the hostess's smile to the design of the menu, is shaped by the imperative to persuade us to spend more money, either on this visit or the next. The pictures in the menu tell us what the food is going to look like, and the text tells us how the food is going to taste.

We have entered into gastronomic hyperreality, a zone of experience where the taste of the food itself melds seamlessly with the sensations conveyed by the marketing messages that surround the food to create a unified experience. Given a product that has virtually no intrinsic qualities, the advertising isn't merely essential to sell the product, it becomes part of the experience of consuming the product.

Coke adds life; to drink Pepsi is to be young, have fun, become part of a generation.

But as the imagery and symbolism that surround the product become richer, the product itself becomes simpler. The infinite variety that characterizes the world of natural kinds—the world in which every apple has a slightly different shape, color, taste—is giving way to a world in which the thing itself—the apple, the hamburger, the cola—has an absolute generic uniformity, becomes the raw matter onto which symbols can be imprinted. The dry, brown patty at the center of a McDonald's hamburger is merely a marker, an unarticulated hook for the commercial message that the McDonald's corporation hangs on it. What is evolving is consumption in purer and purer forms, divorced from any connection to quenching our thirst, satisfying our hunger, or fulfilling any other basic need.

In the postmodern world, it is the experience of consumption that is the source of pleasure, rather than the physical act of eating. Consumption is a ritual act; it is not the intrinsic qualities of the Coke or burger or fries that matter, since these are minimal and generic. The Coke is cold and fizzy and sweet, the burger warm and chewy and oily and salty. What matters is the good feelings that go with the product.

Intrinsic qualities actually get in the way of consumption, because they come up against the natural limits of human capacity, whether it be our capacity for sugar, fiber, calories, or caffeine. Removing the sugar from soft drinks overcomes one obstacle to consumption, but the ultimate consumable may well be the sugar-free, caffeine-free cola. But is sugar-free, caffeine-free Coke still the Real Thing?

THE HIGHER REALITY

None of this means that the force of these advertising messages somehow simply cancels itself out. Rather, they combine to create a messy but coherent reality. It might be tempting to call it an alternative reality, or a higher reality, but in fact, this other reality has interpenetrated the reality of our daily lives to such a degree that they are inseparable.

This higher reality exists in the movies, on television, in the pages of newspapers and magazines, and ultimately, in our heads. Most Americans spend many hours every day in communion with that reality. We are most obviously in contact with that reality when we are sitting in front of our television sets, watching news or entertainment programming, or commercials, or when we go to a movie theater. But we are also in contact with that fantasy world when we visit Disney World or Knott's Berry Farm, or even when we walk into the local McDonald's or Gap or Banana Republic.

It is a world of people who are, for the most part, happier than the people in our own immediate circle of aquaintances. They have better teeth than we do, and they live more exciting lives. They face a variety of problems in their daily lives, but these seem invariably to resolve themselves within the span of half an hour. They often say very funny things, and when they do, laughter echoes mysteriously from nowhere.

An aura surrounds the people who live in this world— whether it is Clint Eastwood or Cindy Crawford or even Roseanne or the local television news anchor. They live life more intensely than we do. It may sound odd at first to say this, but if we accept the idea that at the core of the erotic is the experience of an intensified sense of aliveness, then they are erotic figures.

The aura that surrounds them seems to intensify as the gap that separates our lives from theirs widens. Increasingly the content of their lives is a nostalgic depiction of what is vanishing from ours—they chat with their neighbors, their families are intact, they fall in love.

They are gods. We want to be like them. And they want *us* to be like them, or at least to flatter ourselves that we could be. And the way we can be like them is to buy the products that they consume. Consumption is the bridge between our world and theirs.

To be somebody is to be acknowledged in the image world. The promise of salvation is the promise of passage from this world to the next, and it is a promise that is made every time a commercial shows somebody who could be you—but they have been born again without blemish—living in the luminescent world.

We have been here before. Just as the stained glass of the medieval cathedrals created a shimmering vision of eternal life, the fantasy machinery of the consciousness industry projects an image of a life that is larger, richer, happier than the one we live in. And just as the medieval priests held out the communion wafer as the bridge between the temporal and spiritual worlds, the advertising agencies of today seek to persuade us that we can enter into the shimmering world they project before us by consuming the right products.

Most advertising for food and drink says much less about the intrinsic qualities of the product than it makes promises about how the product can change our lives.

"Brands can create a value proposition and a basis for a relationship by focusing on a particular social or reference group through user imagery," explains David Aaker, author of *Building Strong Brands*. "The possibility of belonging to a user group or obtaining the approval and acceptance of a group may provide an added emotional tie for the consumer. Certainly, the success of Miller Lite's 'Tastes great/less filling' campaign resulted in part from the inclusion of customers in an attractive but accessible group defined by retired star athletes."[8]

Cross-marketing is making the connections between elements of this hyperreality virtually seamless. Buy a Happy

Meal at McDonald's and you can buy a Power Ranger toy as well, and then watch the Power Rangers fight crime on the Saturday morning cartoons, sponsored by McDonald's. Or buy a Meal Deal and you might be an instant winner of a trip to the Olympics, an event that was once a part of the real world but has become a quadrennial marketing festival for Reebok, Kodak, Visa, and McDonald's.

Adults without children may not fully realize how central the McDonald's food experience is in childrens' lives. In a 1991 study, 70 percent of boys six to eight years old, and 75 percent of girls, had eaten at a McDonald's in the past month. Every day 8 percent of all American kids visit a McDonald's. "A large part of the McDonald's success is due to the Happy Meal," explain Selina S. Guber and Jon Berry, authors of *Marketing to and Through Kids,*[9] which promises to tell marketers how to "Tap into the $7 billion kids spend and the $120 billion of purchases they influence." A typical Happy Meal includes a burger, fries, drink, and a toy, packaged in a colorful bag or box, but the key to its success is carefully planned tie-ins to hot toys, movies, or television shows.

If present trends continue, Americans will be spending more and more of their food dollars at chain restaurants in the years to come. Industry consultant Viktor Baker has predicted that in the next decade, full-service chains will overwhelm independent restaurant operations, which have neither the purchasing power nor the marketing dollars to compete.[10] Increasingly that marketing sells the sizzle rather than the steak. The steaks themselves—or more typically, the burgers or grilled chicken breasts—are becoming generic markers, differentiated not by their flavor but by the messages that accompany them. The food arrives on the plate with an interpretation, and the sinful deliciousness promised by the menu prose becomes part of the experience.

The most powerful messages conveyed by the marketers aren't really about the food at all; they are about the consumer him- or herself. Planet Hollywood invites the diner to participate in a world more vivid, more real than the increasingly routinized reality of their daily life: the world projected by Hollywood and Madison Avenue.

Restaurant dining has always had a fantasy dimension, but the nature of the fantasy has changed. In the forties, when the New York restaurant scene was dominated by places like the 21 Club, Sardi's, and the Russian Tea Room, the fantasy was about being somebody in a social world. It mattered where you were seated, because the table you got was a reflection of your status. Luckily for the strivers, the class structure allowed at least a little social mobility. When Cary Grant discreetly slipped a five-dollar bill into the palm of the unctuous mustachioed maître d', it was to assure a good table—one where he could see and be seen.

Today that social world has been replaced by a fantasy world, in which we participate by consuming—not only food but sweatshirts, keychains, and other merchandise. In this way the act of consumption becomes sacramental. Consumption is thus not so much a matter of fulfilling biological needs as an effort to create and maintain a sense of identity by buying symbolically identified goods.

THE TURN TO VIRTUALITY AND PRIVATE PLEASURES

As Americans become more and more absorbed by the fantasy world of virtuality, in which images and reality become inseparably intertwined, the real material world, and particularly the commons, is allowed to fall apart. It becomes increasingly difficult to persuade citizens to support parks and libraries with their taxes because they no longer spend their time there. But the public world doesn't simply deteriorate; it becomes socially toxic. And we respond the same way we do when the environment is chemically toxic: We keep the kids indoors. We don't really want them watching so much television, but at least we know they're safe.

The uglier the neglected world gets, the more we flee to the replacement reality created by Disney, in which every element of our experience is managed, and the more we flee to that reality, the less satisfying the everyday world is. Real women are disappointing to real men, and vice versa, because they don't look and act like the ones in the commercials.

"At the same time that virtuality proliferates and the flesh becomes a resource base for the mediascape the material conditions of virtuality implode," warn political scientists Arthur Kroker and Michael A. Weinstein. "How long can this condition last before there is a crash?"[11]

We Are
What We Eat

Under postmodern conditions, persons exist in a state of continuous construction and reconstruction; it is a world where anything goes that can be negotiated.
—KENNETH J. GERGEN, *THE SATURATED SELF*

Sometimes you feel like a nut, sometimes you don't.
—ADVERTISEMENT FOR PETER PAUL CANDY BARS

If we are what we eat, then what are we? The daily necessity of eating has shaped every culture and civilization, from the earliest tribes of hunter-gatherers to postindustrial societies. The work we must do to nourish ourselves, and the social arrangements we must enter into, shape us as persons. But what happens to the self in a culture that seems to be coming apart at the seams?

Most of us take it for granted that there is such a thing as a human nature that we all share, regardless of what culture or what historical period we live in. "People are people," the saying goes; cultures may vary, but the basic motivations that prompt people to act the way they do are the same.

The contrary view holds that we are to a very large degree the creatures of our culture, and that different cultures and different stages of material development can produce radically different kinds of people.

In this view the reality we live in keeps changing because we keep changing it. And as we change that reality, by establishing trading routes and market towns or by inventing telephones and automobiles, we change ourselves, and what we have the potential to become. Mobile societies produce different kinds of people than static ones. The city, with its diversity of cultures, variety of stimulus, and relative anonymity, creates different kinds of persons than the country village. Literate people have different ways of knowing than illiterate ones. And cultures in turmoil create selves who mirror the society's conflicting forces.

Over the past few centuries, as one era or culture has gradually given way to the next, different kinds of selves have emerged. The nineteenthth century gave us the romantic self, the self of inwardness, passion and soul, argues psychologist Kenneth Gergen. Selfhood was understood to reside in the immortal soul, which was only temporarily incarnated in a physical body. Those who lived their mortal lives in accordance with revealed religious truth were destined to go on to an eternal life, provided that they did not succumb to the passions of the flesh.

Corresponding to each era's construction of the self has been a different ideology of food and diet. In the mid-nineteenth century Sylvester Graham (of Graham cracker flour fame) took the nation by storm with his *Lectures on the Science of Human Life*, in which he advocated a diet of whole grains, vegetables, and pure water, free of spices, salt, pepper, coffee, tea, beef, pork, or ale. "Every individual should as a general rule restrain himself to the smallest quantity which he finds from careful investigation . . . to fully meet the alimentary wants of the vital economy, knowing that whatsoever is more than this is evil."

The goal of proper diet, in Graham's view, wasn't merely good health and long life; Graham also promised that following his diet would enable men and women to "so subdue their sexual propensity as to be able to abstain from connubial commerce and preserve their entire chastity of body, for several months in succession, without the least inconvenience."[1]

Overeating had moral significance for Sylvester Graham and his followers; it was the sin of gluttony, and the moral duty was to resist it lest the soul be corrupted. To be strong we must deny ourselves and delay our gratifications. The cure was abstinence. Today the cure for consumption is consumption. Weight Watchers does not ask you to give up anything, but rather invites you to eat your way to your ideal weight.

The romantic self of Graham's era gave way by the late nineteenth century to a modernist self. As science and technology transformed the landscape, they also become dominant models for understanding both the body and the mind. Humans were machines, whose inner workings could be understood by the new sciences of nutrition and psychology.

As Americans were adjusting to the stresses of an increasingly urbanized way of life, a new disease was discovered, with an appropriately scientific-sounding name, "neurasthenia," whose symptoms consisted mainly of listlessness and a lack of will. George Beard, the physician who popularized neurasthenia, attributed it to constitutional deficiencies and to the generalized weakened condition caused by the demands of middle- and upper-middle-class life.

Patients suffering from this disease could find treatment at the Battle Creek Sanitorium, operated by a dynamic young doctor named John Harvey Kellogg. (Although John Harvey Kellogg invented the cornflake, it was his brother Will who built the Kellogg cereal empire.) Kellogg specialized in such diseases of the rich; seriously ill patients were turned away. At the San (as it was known), Kellogg preached the gospel of "biologic living," restoring his patients on a regimen of grapes, bran, leafy green vegetables and daily enemas (to prevent putrefaction of food in the bowels, which could cause the debilitating condition known as autointoxication). Alcohol, tobacco, coffee, and tea were forbidden, red meat and rich desserts frowned upon.

As unappetizing as this may sound, it was the perfect diet for the Victorian self, which admired character, discipline, and self-control. Food that actually tasted good would be an invitation to dangerous self-indulgence. When the Kelloggs chief rival C. W. Post introduced Grape-Nuts in 1899, he didn't advertise their good taste; rather, he advertised them as "the most scientific food in the world."

C. W. Post's invocations of science may have lacked credibility, but over the decades that followed, a nutrition establishment came into being and consolidated its authority in matters of nutritional truth. At the turn of the century the new field of domestic science was born, where women excluded from the masculine domain of "real" science taught and were taught a gospel of good nutrition that framed the question of what to eat within a larger project of self-improvement and self-control. "The naked act of eating was little more than unavoidable as far as gently raised women of their era were concerned, and was not to be considered a pleasure except with great discretion," writes food historian Laura Shapiro:

> Domestic scientists were inspired by the nutritive properties of food, by its abilities to promote phys-

ical, social, and, they believed, moral growth. . . .
They did understand very well that many people
enjoyed eating; this presented still another challenge. Food was powerful, it could draw forth cravings and greedy desires which had to ɒe met with a
firm hand.[2]

SOURCES OF THE SELF

There are elements of both the romantic and the modern in
the way people think about their own identities today, and
in the ways we approach food. The appeal of soul food and
comfort food, with their promise of spiritual nourishment, is
essentially romantic in its origins, while the intensified
awareness of calories and cholesterol is a legacy of the modernist worldview. But the emergence of America's new Pleasure Island food culture, with all its pleasures and dangers,
would not have been possible without the emergence of a
new postmodern self, attuned not to production and self-
denial but rather to consumption and gratification.

Today, says psychologist Gergen, "both the romantic
and the modern views about the self are falling into disuse
and the social arrangements that they support are eroding."
The old ideal of a personality that remained constant in
every situation has gradually given way to the ideal of a
more flexible character, a "minimal self," as cultural historian Christopher Lasch termed it.[3] This flexible character
adapts more readily to the moral and psychological
demands of the corporate environment, and reinvents itself
more easily as career changes require.

THE FRAGMENTATION OF THE SELF

But even this minimal self is proving difficult to sustain. The
romantic era and the modernist era each had a sort of
internal coherence, and so did the persons they produced.
In the postmodern era in which we live, the Enlightenment's

grand vision of a world ruled by reason has largely col-
lapsed, replaced by a competing cacophony of visions.

Today the more prophetically inclined postmoderns,
starting with French intellectual Michel Foucault, are proclaiming the disappearance of the self. We are simply the
intersections of competing discourses, as they like to say,
and the messages of these discourses, with which we are
constantly bombarded, are so conflicting that the task of
weaving them together into a coherent whole is simply
hopeless.

"Social saturation furnishes us with a multiplicity of incoherent and unrelated languages of the self," argues Gergen.

> For everything we "know to be true" about ourselves,
> other voices within respond with doubt and even
> derision. The fragmentation of self-conceptions cor-
> responds to a multiplicity of incoherent and discon-
> nected relationships. These relationships pull us in
> myriad directions, inviting us to play such a variety of
> roles that the very concept of an "authentic self" with
> knowable characteristics recedes from view. The fully
> saturated self becomes no self at all.[4]

Emblematic of the new world of eating is the all-you-can-
eat buffet. Gone is any order of eating. The implicit moral
structure of the meal, remembered from childhood—first
you eat your vegetables, and then you get your dessert—is
overthrown. You can start with dessert if you like, and you
can have as much as you want. If you have multiple selves
to feed, the buffet is the ideal solution: a stop at the salad
bar for your more health-conscious side, and a trip to the
carving station for the part of you that craves red meat. (At
the end of the meal, the two of you will have to go home in
the same body, but that's not the immediate problem.)

We aren't simply saturated selves, as Gergen argues,

but most of us are, in varying degrees, fragmented selves. Multiple-personality disorder, once a medical rarity, has become much more common. There is considerable evidence that schizophrenia has a strong biological component, but psychologist Louis Sass argues persuasively that it is also a disease of modernity. One of the most characteristic symptoms of schizophrenia is an intensified level of self-awareness, and that is also a basic characteristic of modern life: We are constantly being monitored and measured, and are constantly monitoring and measuring ourselves. As markets are increased by the manufacture of discontent, the areas in which we must monitor ourselves expand: Our weight must be more closely monitored, and now also our cholesterol levels, our fat intake, our facial hair.

In olden days, or so the theory goes, not only were we not nearly as self-conscious about what we ate, but we were also much less self-conscious about who we were. We derived our identities from the groups to which we belonged and the things that we produced. Gradually our culture has moved in the direction of a radical individualism. We have shifted to defining ourselves in terms of what we consume.

THE INCREDIBLE SHRINKING SELF

There is a pattern to this succession of selves, and an underlying logic. Each successive self becomes smaller. Whereas the postwar self of the early fifties defined itself in terms of work and family, the sexual revolution and the changing realities of the workplace have made both our work and family roles more tenuous parts of our identities. Ethnicity and geography also play more marginal roles in our sense of self; most middle-class Americans are too mobile to develop a strong sense of being from a place, and the current revival of ethnic consciousness is for most Americans merely another form of nostalgia, expressed by certain tokens rather than participation in a fully articulated way of life.

The boundaries of the contemporary self have shrunk to the perimeters of our bodies, which often feel like all that holds the fragmented elements of our identity together.

The underlying logic of this progression of selves is the logic of I-It, to use the philosopher Martin Buber's term. The history of our culture is a history of an ever-sharpening dualism between subject and object, developing over centuries and even millennia. Our earliest ancestors lived in an enchanted world, in which spirit was everywhere: in trees, rocks, and all the forms of animal world. In adopting a scientific worldview, we have learned—or perhaps we should say, come to believe—that the things in the world that we once saw as spirit filled are mere matter. This quest for mastery has allowed us to objectify the physical world, to break it down and reassemble it, and we have proceeded to do the same thing to our relations to animals, and ultimately to everyone, including ourselves.

Consumerism treats everything in the world as stuff—not just the trees and rocks and mountains, which can be consumed as experiences or else made into something that can be consumed— but also animals and people. And ultimately we pay a terrible price for this way of seeing the world, not only in terms of what it does to the world but also in terms of what it does to us. It leads ultimately to a solipsistic universe. The oft-expressed wish that men should stop objectifying women (and vice versa) is well intended but extremely difficult to realize when we are in the grip of a worldview in which we objectify everything. We can understand what a kinder, gentler form of objectification would be, but we have great difficulty understanding a way of connecting that isn't objectifying at all.

The fragmentation of the self that we experience may be nothing more than the ultimate stage of this dynamic of objectification. The self itself is chopped up into ever-smaller pieces, which can be modified, perfected, or abandoned.

THE ROOTLESS SELF

There was a time when most people lived in relatively stable and homogeneous communities, in which each individual's life was enmeshed in a network of relationships that often lasted an entire lifetime. The central facts of your life were likely to be common knowledge within the community. Your station and its duties were defined largely by your birth. If you were the baker's son, you would likely become a baker, too, and if you were the baker's daughter, you would likely become someone's wife and somebody's mother and the manager of a domestic economy. The nature of these roles was clearly modeled within the community, and changed only very slowly over time.

Your sense of who you were was derived from what you produced, whether it was bread, or chairs or houses, or children and meals for the family table. Your esteem in the community was likely to be a function of how skilled you were at doing this work.

There is little point in disputing whether this way of life was a rich source of selfhood or a suffocating trap; it could be either and was often both. But clearly, for better or for worse, it established as fixed many of the core elements of personal identity that are now, for many individuals, undefined or in perpetual flux.

Changes in the way work is organized have undermined our productive activities as a source of identity. Twenty-five years ago sociologists and philosophers were intensely focused on the problem of alienation in modern society. Underlying this notion was the idea that there was a true self within each person that he or she could realize through creative activity. The idea, which goes back to Marx, is that we could realize our essential human nature by seeing it reflected in the things that we produce. Alienation came about when production shifted from the skilled artisan to the unskilled tender of automated production equipment.

But the self that is presented to the customer at the Rainforest Cafe or the retro diner Ed Debevic's is a scripted facade. Is there a lonely and isolated soul behind the mask, silently crying out, But that's not who I really am!? Unlikely. An earlier, more romantic generation might have had a sense of alienation, a sense that the true self was being smothered, but the younger generation senses that all we are is the roles that we play, and it's really rather nice to be given a role that's scripted and easy to follow, and where the uniforms are provided by the company.

Today the concern over losing touch with that inner self has vanished; the romantic dream of self-realization through creative activity has given way to a way of life in which we find meaning through consumption.

THE FAMILY AS SOURCE OF SELFHOOD

Another traditionally important source of our sense of self has been the circles of social connectedness in which we participate, of which the most intimate was the family. A web of law, custom, and economic necessity held families together throughout a lifetime: The jobs of nurturing infants, raising children, preparing the next generation to gain its livelihood, and taking care of the aged in their declining years bound families together.

Today all those webs of family connectedness have been systematically weakened. In households where the adults work outside the home, the work of nurturing the children is in large part done for hire by others, in day care centers or by nannies in the home, and only rarely by relatives. The extended family has become a rarity, and the traditional nuclear family frequently held forth as an ideal is actually a rarity, too. True family intimacy is something we are more likely to encounter on television or in the movies than in real life; according to one estimate, American parents have as little as thirty seconds a day of intimate conversation with their children.

The bonds between fathers and their children have been strained ever since the Industrial Revolution, which took fathers out of the home and away from routine intimate contact with their children. The breakdown of the legal and social barriers to divorce, and the increase in childbirth outside marriage, are resulting in a growing number of children raised without fathers. But even fathers who live in the same houses as their children are largely absent from their lives, as the job of raising the children falls disproportionately on their mothers or on outsiders, or gets done by the television set. One University of Michigan study found that on weekends, fathers spend less than eight minutes talking to their children.[5]

Family arrangements change almost as frequently as careers. Children don't just leave the family home, they frequently leave the hometown as well, staying connected by telephone and holiday visits. (Does this make the telephone and the airplane technologies of connection or of separation?) Social security has removed the traditional necessity, still prevalent in traditional cultures, to produce offspring who will provide for you in your old age, and with it the bonds of moral obligation traditionally transmitted by the culture. In the final stages of life, parents are more likely to be taken care of by nursing home staff than by their children.

Even when parents are present in their children's lives, they are often no longer acceptable role models. The generation of women who stayed home to raise their children has produced a generation of daughters who themselves are reaching, or have reached, adulthood. Whether they view their mothers' choice with envy, as a more attractive alternative to the drudgery of the workplace, or as a mistaken sacrifice of the opportunity for self-realization through a career, this much is clear: For the vast majority, following in their footsteps is no longer an option. And for the generation of sons whose fathers supported their families on a single income, and whose wives met them at the end of a working day with a kiss and a hot dinner, neither their fathers' accomplishments nor their rewards are in reach.

THE LOSS OF THE PUBLIC WORLD

The larger circles of social connectedness are also in disrepair. Besides the family and the world of work, another important source of identity has traditionally been our participation in the life of a community. But over the last three decades, while the world of private gastronomic pleasures has exploded, the web of human association has been slowly but steadily unraveling.

For many of our ancestors, and perhaps even for ourselves in the past, our primary challenge was to struggle against the constraints that our community placed upon us, the barriers that it imposed to freedom and self-realization. In some cases people rebelled against the norms that dictated what they could study, what they could become, how they could worship, whom they could love or marry.

Today, however, the most common complaint is not of too much community, but too little. Political scientist Robert Putnam has documented a dramatic decline over the last twenty years in "social capital . . . the features of social organization such as networks, norms and social trust that facilitate coordination and cooperation for social trust." Between the early 1960s and 1990, voter turnout declined by nearly a quarter. Americans attend far fewer public meetings than they once did. Union membership has fallen by more than half. Participation in parent-teacher associations has declined from twelve million in 1964 to seven million now. Volunteerism is also in steep decline; the Boy Scouts attract 26 percent fewer volunteers than in 1970, and the Red Cross has suffered a 61 percent decline.

Membership in the Masons, Jaycees, and Lions is also down sharply. The reasons for their decline are various, but the consequence is that we know each other less well and have less occasion to develop the webs of interdependence that give rise to a moral order.

Political scientists worry about the long-term impact of this decline on the viability of democratic institutions. But the same institutions that give voice to common interests and shape the political dialogue also give shape to the identities of their participants. Putnam makes this claim cautiously: "Dense networks of interaction probably broaden the participants sense of self, developing the 'I' into the 'we'."

His research is controversial; some have suggested that the web of social interconnections has merely assumed new forms, specifically, the rise of therapeutic and self-help groups, such as AA and Al-Anon. This may or may not be true, but in any case these new forms of connection do not sustain the old moral order. In fact, the therapeutic culture in most instances specifically rejects the vocabulary of morality.

Today most Americans live relatively anonymous lives. We still call the places where we live "neighborhoods" or "communities," but increasingly they are neither. Whereas they once were the centers of economic and social life for the people who lived in them, today they are frequently little more than bedroom communities. Between 1974 and 1993 the number of Americans who spent a social evening with a neighbor more than once a year declined from 72 to 61 percent.

If someone asks you, "Where do you live?" you are likely to answer with the name of a neighborhood, or a nearby geographic landmark. But if you give the question a sharper focus and ask yourself "And do I really live there?" then the answer becomes more vexing. Most of us can't claim to really live in the neighborhoods where we sleep. Few of us have the time to take part in the life of the community, and in many cases, there is no community life to take part in. To varying degrees many of us can say of our neighborhoods what Gertrude Stein said of Oakland: "There is no there there."

Bodenständigkeit is German philosopher Martin Heidegger's term for the sense of being rooted in a place. It is this connection to a place that grounds us in Being, Heidegger claimed, and even if you don't buy into the existential mumbo-jumbo, it's not hard to understand the underlying insight: People who have no rootedness to a place are tumbleweeds, blown about on the currents of the zeitgeist. You have to be somebody, from somewhere, to know who you are.

The real threat virtuality poses to our humanity comes from its undermining of our locatedness. To reroot ourselves in the particularity of our place requires resisting the onslaught of interchangable symbols. It means eating the food that can only come from where you live, that has the particularities of the land and the people and the history imprinted on it. And if you can't afford that, you are truly poor.

We are today in a transitional period, in which we still live with a legacy of stories about a richer life, with more fulfilling possibilities for human connection. And we experience profound disappointment with the lack of those connections in our lives. Those feelings are amplified when we see depictions of that rich social life in movies and on television. Evolutionary psychologists speculate that a longing for that kind of connectedness is somehow bred into our genes.[6] True or not, it certainly seems possible that in another generation or two, as the people who have memories of sitting on a porch or stoop in a lively neighborhood on a hot summer day disappear, their stories may disappear as well, and if a wish for connectedness *is* bred into our genes, all that may remain is an inchoate but painful longing.

The new technologies of the automobile, television, and computer have proved to be technologies of isolation. The chance pedestrian encounters that were part of the fabric of urban neighborhood life are rare occurrences in the suburban neighborhoods where most Americans now live. Instead of walking to the corner store, we drive to the mall, which may be several miles away. (Many newer suburban communities don't even have sidewalks.) Thanks to the electric garage door opener, it has become possible to go from our cars into our homes without ever setting foot in our neighborhoods.

Television isolates as well: Americans watch television an average of twenty-eight hours a week, and that is time they are not spending communicating with one another. Even the refrigerator and the air conditioner work as isolating technologies: We shop for our groceries once a week instead of daily, and we now spend the hottest days of summer in the climate-controlled comfort of our living rooms instead of sitting on the front stoop, talking to our neighbors.

"This decline of the civic sphere, of the voluntary and informal associations that constitute the underbrush in the ecology of public life, has been paralleled by the rise of the bureaucratic sphere," argues community organizer John McKnight.[7] More and more of the work that was once done within the informal sphere is now done by bureaucracies: the work of teaching, healing, policing, punishing, nurturing.

"We are known to each of these bureaucracies only in a partial aspect: as patients, victims, perpetrators, students. It is only within the informal sector that we are known more fully, and that our whole identity is acknowledged."

In the days before so much of our entertainment came packaged in commodity form, on television, in the movies, on videotapes and CDs, or on the Internet, it was the custom among humans to entertain themselves by making music, playing games, or telling stories. Knowing how to do these things was one of the skills that people learned by being part of a society. Learning to make music or tell stories was one of the ways in which they realized their potential as human beings, and at the same time was a means of articulating relationships with other people.

Today, since we have created technologies that can make our music and tell our stories for us, our ability to do those things for ourselves is in decline. We can buy greeting cards that articulate the appropriate sentiments for all occasions, but we seem to be increasingly unable to articulate—and perhaps even to feel—those emotions ourselves. That may explain the increasing market for greeting cards that express an ironic or humorous tone. Our relations to one another are sufficiently ambiguous to make direct expressions of emotion seem dangerous.

Pinocchio lost his humanity—symbolized by the ability to speak—when he became a consumer. It is a loss that teachers also report in students who have spent the better part of their childhood staring at a television set, mesmerized by an ongoing stream of images. The ability to speak, beyond grunts and simple utterances, is contingent on a way of life that engages our humanity more fully. The more efficiently we are adapted to roles in production processes, the less of that capacity to articulate will we have occasion to develop and draw on.

Another source of that loss of articulateness is the spread of the preinterpreted experience. The more our world is made up of objects whose meaning is already defined, the less opportunity there is for us to engage and interpret it imaginatively.

SMALLER LIVES

As the public world disintegrates, we live smaller lives. Most Americans, regardless of how materially affluent they may be, have social lives that are, by comparison with those of the average Bangladeshi villager or Albanian peasant, quite impoverished. Is there anyone beyond your immediate family—or even in your immediate family—who can tell a story about you? Can you tell a story about yourself? Does anyone really know who you are? We may possess more goods, but we live smaller lives.

Another missing piece of our selfhood, for many Americans, is the erotic. In a culture that objectifies everything, even the objects of our passion become objects, and the union we yearn for—the union that transcends our own boundaries—becomes increasingly difficult to achieve. Although our culture is saturated with sexualized imagery of women, men, food, automobiles, and virtually everything else, the erotic energy of the culture has rarely felt so depleted.

In his recent book, *Intimate Terrorism: The Deterioration of Erotic Life*, psychotherapist Michael Vincent Miller traces this depletion to the loss of a larger context of community and shared meanings within which individual relationships traditionally were embedded:

> Relations between men and women in the past may have been overloaded with obligation and practicality. But they were also strengthened by bonds more durable than love itself can forge. Such bonds fortified the erotic connection because they gave it purposes beyond itself. A man and a woman used to make love in a cosmos filled with widely shared

communal and religious beliefs. Now they make love only in a bed, to which they bring all their anxieties and dreams. That can be a fulfilling experience for a time, but it's still not enough to sustain a lasting intimacy.[8]

FEEDING THE EMPTY SELF

It has become a cliché to say that we live in a consumer society, but the full implications of this fact aren't often spelled out. It means not merely that the society is characterized by high levels of consumption but that being consumers increasingly defines who we are as individuals. Consumption is not only the activity through which we seek satisfaction but also the one through which we construct our own identities. Whether it's Acuras, Rolexes, Levi's 501s, Pepsis, or Big Macs, every choice we make about what we consume makes a statement about who we are, and no one hears that statement louder than we do ourselves. Choices of material goods become the idiom through which we elaborate our selves and position ourselves socially.

As psychoanalyst Philip Cushman explains: "The predominant self in the post–World War II era needed to be configured in such a way as to adapt to, and in fact promote, consumerism. The consumer society was achieved through the constructing of a self that was empty, a self that feels naturally and irresistibly driven to consume in order to fill up the emptiness."[9]

The most simplistic explanations of compulsive eating suggest that he or she who does it just enjoys food too much to exercise self-control. But compulsive eaters get little gustatory pleasure from the food they eat; rather, they wolf (or gobble) their food down, as if driven not by a desire for pleasure but the need to fill an inner emptiness.

This inner emptiness is the modern—or rather, postmodern— condition. The central promise of a consumer culture is that we can find fulfillment through consumption. We have an economy that depends on the constant consumption of goods and services. The hunger itself must be manufactured, as much as the foods that are supposed to satisfy it.

"In the post–World War II era in the United States the shape of the cultural landscape has configured the self of the upper and middle classes into a particular kind of masterful, bounded self: the empty self," writes Cushman.

> By this I mean a self that experiences a significant absence of community, tradition, and shared meaning—a self that experiences these social absences and their consequences "interiorly" as a lack of personal conviction and worth; a self that embodies the absences, loneliness and disappointments of life as a chronic and undifferentiated emotional hunger. Without the empty self, America's consumer-based economy would be inconceivable.[10]

Anxieties about food and eating today bear a striking resemblance to the anxieties about sexuality in the fifties. Sexuality became a focal point then because it was a time when the nature of the relationship between men and women was up for grabs. It was up for grabs because a fundamental rupture in the traditional relationship between men and women was under way. This splitting off was especially threatening to women, for whom it represented a loss, not only of their traditional role, but also of economic security.

In the same way food has become invested with emotional power because it too has been invested with powerful emotional symbolism. But what chasm is it that we seek to bridge this time? Who is it that we are split off from?

Ourselves. We have achieved a degree of self-consciousness and fragmentation unprecedented in the history of our species. While one set of technologies isolates us from other humans—for example, television, the automobile, and all those technologies that promote self-sufficiency, such as the microwave oven, the home washing machine, the refrigerator, and the air conditioner—another set of technologies gives us new tools for self-objectification: the bathroom scale, the Nautilus machine, the psychological theories of everyone from Wayne Dyer to Sigmund Freud, and the constant bombardment of images that portray what we should look like.

In the new reality it is increasingly difficult to have satisfactory intimate relationships with others, so we turn more and more to the effort to have a satisfactory relationship with ourselves, based on such ideas as self-esteem.

This sense of fragmentation is a natural stimulus to overeating. What better way to reconnect to yourself than by nurturing yourself? What better way to compensate for the absence of nurturing relationships than to feed yourself? The old psychobabble about learning to be your own best friend wouldn't make much sense if it didn't speak to the sense of an internal splitting. And a whole category of food products and advertising has developed that plays off of this need for inner healing, by delivering the key message in a way that you can be good to yourself.

Sweet Rewards, General Mills's new line of fat-free treats, are not intended as presents for your pet or your lover, but as a reward you give yourself. It isn't clear what you are rewarding yourself for, but maybe that isn't the point. Perhaps the point is simply to summon back to memory the feelings of an earlier and less complicated time, when you got rewarded for doing your homework.

Food was, in our earliest life, the bridge reconnecting us to the person who nurtured us. Today, especially for people who must nurture themselves, eating can create a feeling, albeit only a temporary one, of wholeness and connectedness.

While our social worlds have become impoverished, our mental worlds have seen a population increase: We all carry around inside our heads, to varying degrees, a little homunculus who keeps an observing eye on us, telling us whether we are too fat or too flabby. To counteract this cruel little inspector general, we are encouraged to make a little more space inside our heads for other, friendlier spirits: Jane Hirschmann and Carol Munter, authors of *When Women Stop Hating Their Bodies*, encourage us to develop a new internal caretaker who talks back when the little homunculus speaks to us too harshly.[11]

To the degree that our customs of eating are part of the set of practices that give order to our lives, the collapse of these coherent orders of eating can be seen as a significant causative factor in the emergence of the de-centered, post-modern self.

As the pace of change in our lives accelerates, and as the boundaries that once separated different communities into coherent and homogeneous entities disintegrate, casting us all helter-skelter into a babel of confused and conflicting values and stories—well, it's at times like this that a guy or a gal wants something solid to bite into, like maybe a big, juicy hamburger.

If being anxious makes you want to eat, then you are not alone. These are anxious times, and if eating for comfort weren't already a natural impulse under the circumstances, there is the added encouragement provided by a whole category of food products and advertisements designed to promote the food-comfort connection. Nothing's quite as loving as something from the oven, and Pillsbury says it best.

AND NOW, A WORD FROM OUR SPONSOR

If consumerism is a solution to the problem of the self—that is, the problem of creating an identity in a time when all the old sources of identity are in disarray, then it is also a solution to a problem of the economy. The development of a consumer society was a response to a recurring problem in capitalist economies: the social instability produced by cyclical swings in the economy. The Great Depression was only the most recent of these, from which only World War II provided an escape. Wars are very effective ways of stimulating high levels of employment and production, and of using up that production rapidly and efficiently, thereby ensuring an ongoing need for more production.

But once World War II was over, in order to avoid another depression, new ways had to be found to ensure sustained high levels of production and consumption. The solution lay in advertising.

"Advertising is the culture developed to expedite the central problem of capitalism: the distribution of surplus goods," says social critic James Twitchell.[12] True enough, but we could equally well turn that observation on its head: Our contemporary culture, whether high or avant garde or popular, is one developed by advertising. To take full account of the impact of advertising on our world, it is necessary to consider not only the television commercial, newspaper and magazine advertisements, billboards and bus placards, and sponsored buildings, exhibits, and championships, but also the content of all these, which, from the marketer's perspective, are merely ways to attract our attention to the most important message.

Advertising and the empty self sustain each other. "Because the postwar emptiness is, in part an absense of communal beliefs and traditions, individuals in this era are particularly vulnerable to influence from cultural institutions such as advertising that emanates authority and certainty," argues Cushman. "The lifestyle solution is advertising's cure for the empty self."

One crucial fact about the vast outpouring of the consciousness industry that produces our popular culture is that it is predominantly a sponsored culture. Nearly every message we receive through the media is sponsored, presented by some entity that seeks to persuade or induce us to take some action in response.

By one estimate the average American sees about one hundred television commercials, and a total of sixteen thousand commercial messages a day—in forms ranging from billboards and magazine ads to "product placements" to corporate logos. Taken together these ads construct an image of reality. But they are not the only source of our image of this world. It comes to us on every page of most of the magazines we read, whether *Playboy* or *Road & Track* or *Martha Stewart Living.*

Today television is our culture. It takes up more of our free waking hours than any other activity—far more time than most Americans spend engaged in sports, talking to friends or family, making love, or eating. In fact, many Americans eat, and even make love, while watching television, or at least with the television glowing in the background. The comedy troupe Firesign Theater asked the question, How can you be in two places at once when you are really nowhere at all? Television is the answer.

An analysis of messages about food and eating behavior on prime-time television found that food was referred to an average of 4.8 times every half hour, not counting commercials. Most references were to non-nutritious consumables such as coffee, alcohol, sweets, and salty snacks. Thirty-five percent of commercials seen during the period studied were for food, primarily fast-food restaurants.[13]

Critic Neal Postman has used a McDonald's commercial to illustrate the way in which television has transformed and debased public discourse. In a word-centered culture, propositions play a central role. Propositions have a logical structure, and make assertions about the nature of reality that can be tested and judged true or false. Television marks a turn away from a word-based society—the McDonald's commercial presents an image that can be attractive or repellent, but never true or false.

In a culture dominated by the epistemology of television, storytelling disappears. And since traditional morality depends on storytelling, it is undermined. Traditional morality tells a story about actors, that relates actors to events in such ways that they can be held accountable. But without storytelling, traditional morality disappears. In its place we have a morality centered on the image: If you look good, you are good; if you look bad, that is, fat, you are bad. This creates a great opening for food products that let you sin without suffering the consequences.

In television programs and movies, narrative is increasingly secondary to the visual display, and the succession of disconnected but emotionally charged events, whether they be action sequences, one-liners, or scenes of sexual display. News programs, which purport to convey a picture of reality, are particularly fragmented, breaking the world up into ever more rapid sequences of sound bites and dramatic images. This dominance of the image is most obvious in visual media such as television and film, but its impact has transformed magazines and newspapers as well.

In place of narrative or argument, the messages of the sponsored culture offer us repeated sequences of stimulation and catharsis. This is particularly true in commercial television. "The chief expectation of the sponsored life is that there will and always should be regular blips of excitement and resolution, the frequency of which is determined by money," writes *Village Voice* media critic Leslie Savan:

> We begin to pulse to the beat, the one-two beat, that moves most ads: problem/solution, old/new, Brand X/hero brand, desire/gratification. In order to dance to the rhythm, we adjust other expectations a little

here, a little there: Our notions of what's desirable behavior, our lust for novelty, even our vision of the perfect love affair or thrilling adventure adapt to the mass consensus coaxed out by marketing.[14]

One might expect that this vast industry would add up to nothing more than cacophony, a babel of competing and conflicting claims. In a sense this is true. We live in a world so saturated with these messages that it becomes increasingly difficult to achieve the critical distance necessary to perceive how they affect us and our world.

"The sponsored life is born when commercial culture sells our own experiences back to us," says Savan. "It grows as those experiences are then reconstituted inside us, mixing the most intimate processes of individual thought with commercial values, rhythms and expectations. . . . The viewer who lives the sponsored life—and that is most of us to one degree or the other—is slowly recreated in the ad's image."

In our consumer society, consumption is no longer centered on meeting basic needs for food, clothing, and shelter. Rather, it is the way we create and maintain a sense of identity. The acquisition and display of goods becomes the vocabulary through which we proclaim to others, and to ourselves, who we are. "People try to become the being they desire to be by consuming the items that they imagine will help to create and sustain their idea of themselves, their image, their identity," says sociologist Robert Bocock. "Clothes, perfumes, cars, food and drink all may play a role in this process. They *signify* that someone is *x* or *y* to the person themselves and to others who share the same code of signifiers, the same system of signs/symbols."[15]

The message that equates who you are with what you consume is everywhere—in television commercials and magazine advertisements, on billboards and bus placards, in popular novels and films, and in the looks we give each other as we pass on the street.

Taken all together these messages add up to a plausible answer to the age-old question about the meaning of life: As a popular bumper sticker puts it: HE WHO DIES WITH THE MOST TOYS WINS. Plausible, but ultimately not convincing, because for all of our consumption, we are never quite satisfied. If we were, the game would come to an end.

5

Food, Sex, and the New Morality

Eat & eat & eat & eat
eat & eat & eat & eat
eat & eat & eat & eat
& not feel the least bit guilty.
—Print ad for Orville Redenbacher's
reduced fat Smart-Pop popcorn

If it's the next best thing to sex,
you must be having really good sex.
—Print ad for Consorzio Vignette vinegar

If it is remarkable how riddled with guilt our relationship with food has become, it is even more noteworthy how much our morality has become centered on food. The word "sinful" is hardly ever used today except in connection with dessert. It would be wrong to dismiss this as mere metaphor: According to one recent study, single women who have affairs with married men are generally untroubled by feelings of guilt; by contrast, many dieters feel powerful feelings of guilt and self-loathing after succumbing to the temptations of Häagen-Dazs.

The cover of a popular women's magazine lures readers with a headline that promises to reveal the "seven sex sins you should commit." Inside the author proposes: "If eating dessert was the last serious sin you committed, then these seven sex suggestions may inspire you to drop your fork." The suggestions range from renting erotic movies and shaving each other's pubic hair to having "sex with someone you're only attracted to physically. . . . So, if you're single and armed with condoms, there's no reason you have to wait around for Prince Charming to get a bit of nooky."[1] An excess of cheesecake, however, is a more serious matter.

Waiting around for Prince Charming is probably hopeless anyway, suggests an advertisement for I Can't Believe It's Not Butter!, but there are other paths to pleasure. "Just when you thought your fantasy was out of reach, we put it at your fingertips," proclaims the ad, which shows supermodel Fabio reclining in the background, and a sumptuous feast of roast turkey and poached salmon in the foreground. Candles, roses, and a bottle of the butter-flavored spray complete the scene. "Even Fabio can't compete with I Can't Believe It's Not Butter! Spray, the easy way to get fresh butter taste in each serving, without any fat or calories."

In much of our society, sexuality is regarded as a private matter beyond morality's reach. Public attitudes about extramarital sex and homosexuality have changed radically over the past three decades. The stigma once attached to out-of-wedlock pregnancies and births has largely disappeared. A San Francisco organization of prostitutes gave itself the acronym COYOTE, short for "Come Off Your Old Tired Ethics." So why, at a time when morality is in retreat in almost every other sphere, has food become so morally problematic?

Here's a theory: The old morality, in which sexuality was central, has been replaced by a new morality centered on the body. Is it mere coincidence that while participation in

the Catholic sacrament of confession has declined dramatically, millions of Americans now pay to participate in that
commercial ritual of self-disclosure, the weekly Weight
Watchers weigh-in?

"Dear old Freud's id is no longer locked away in the un-
or sub-conscious," says Carole Shaw, editor in chief of *Big
Beautiful Woman*.

> Everything the id ever whispered can be seen,
> heard, and talked about on network and cable TV. So
> the id is out in the open. The EAT is what is only
> whispered about, fantasized about and occasionally
> and secretly indulged in (the way sex used to be)
> with a good deal of morning-after guilt.
>
> "With sex at least you know the score. You either
> have it or you don't. But with food, just a little—not
> even a whole lot—can cause the guilt and remorse
> we used to have about infidelity or dishonesty, or—
> heavens!—impropriety (does anyone even know or
> use that word today?).[2]

In a consumer society, it is what we consume, rather
than how we connect to the social world, that is most central to our identities. Some of us take the fact that we avoid
red meat or can distinguish a cabernet sauvignon from a
pinot noir to be important indicators of who we are, and of
how we are different from or better than others. And in a
culture in which consuming rather than connecting is the
central motivating force, it is only natural that eating has
more erotic potential than sex. Small wonder, then, that
eating has also become more morally troublesome.

Anything can be eroticized. We most often think of eroticism as connected to sex, but the focus of erotic attention
can be nearly anything: parts of the body, kinds of bodies—
very fat or very thin—or even mannerisms—a toughness

or vulnerability. If the core of eroticism is a heightened sense of aliveness, then different things can provoke it for different people, depending on their culture and individual history; for some it is wealth that is erotic, for others symbols of power or domination.

Food today is beautiful and dangerous in the same way that sex once was. Food stylists lavish the same careful attention on the displays photographed for glossy food magazines that Hugh Hefner's retouch artists devote to creating the sexual images of women that appear in *Playboy*. Just as sex was once surrounded by mystery, danger, and the promise of passion and fulfillment, food is now the forbidden fruit, the locus of fear and longing. In the fifties, good girls didn't have sex; today good girls don't have chocolate: "The fat woman is today's equivalent of yesterday's bad girl," write Rosalyn Meadow and Lillie Weiss.

While food has been sexualized, sex has been dissected—autopsied, one might almost say. Broken down into its constituent parts, analyzed, and labeled, its mystery has disappeared. As gender relations have become more self-conscious and problematic, the joy of sex has been undermined by anger, anxiety, and the struggle for power.

In the fifties, according to Meadow and Weiss:

> In spite of the dreaded consequences of losing control sexually, women continued to fantasize about the pleasures of the forbidden fruit, dreaming about giving in to their passions and experiencing the ultimate in ecstasy. . . . Sexual fantasies fueled the imagination, and women became obsessed with having sexual intercourse.
>
> Sex was fraught with danger and excitement and was always on women's minds, so that they could hardly wait for the day when they could come together with their lovers.

Today, while sex has lost much of its mystery and allure, "food advertisements in print and on television tantalize women and fuel their consuming passions for forbidden foods. . . ."[3]

In the fifties a woman who succumbed to her passions was stigmatized socially. A girl with a reputation to protect could always deny the rumors, unless, of course, she became pregnant, in which case her sinfulness would become plain for all to see. Today a woman who succumbs to her desire for food is stigmatized. Women can avoid this stigma by secretly going away to a bathroom and purging themselves of the potential evidence of their transgression, or they can indulge in sugar-free soft-drinks and fat-free snacks (the gastronomic equivalent of heavy petting). But if the evidence of their weakness becomes evident in the shape of their bodies, then they are ostracized.

Sex has lost its promise. In the fifties and sixties, sex was still connected to romance, understood as a merging of two souls into a sort of mystical union. But, starting in the late sixties, both theory and practice turned against that ideal. Hard experience taught women and men—but especially women—that romance was a con. Once the honeymoon was over, millions of American women found themselves asking, with Peggy Lee and Betty Friedan, "Is That All There Is?"

At the same time there was a theoretical assault on the ideal of two hearts merging. This urge to merge was pathologized in therapy as codependency, or as evidence of "boundary problems." Wedding ceremonies of the seventies (and no doubt to this day) sometimes included a reading from Kahlil Gibran, advising couples that, like two trees, they will not thrive if they are planted too close together.

In the nineties sex is still pervasive in advertising and entertainment, but this time around, it has very little to do with romance. What is eroticized is domination. In adver-

tising, women—and often more specifically their breasts—
are trophies in a big-game hunt. Sex becomes a form of
consumption.

Eating and sex are increasingly becoming solitary pur-
suits. In the days when meal preparation was a much more
arduous and time-consuming task than it is today the family
meal was a custom dictated by necessity. Today, when prepared foods make up a large part of the daily diet for many
American families, it is no inconvenience for each member
of the household to eat according to his or her own
schedule.

The strong social sanctions that once existed against
solitary sex have been overthrown by the sexual revolution. A handyman who does routine maintenance in a large
apartment complex reports seeing by many bedsides the
appurtenances of onanism: *Playboy* or *Playgirl* magazine, a
jar of petroleum jelly, a box of tissues. Two-person sexuality
is fraught with danger, and anger, and disappointment (a
bestseller of the eighties, *Why Cucumbers Are Better Than*
Men, captured the bitterness of this disappointment), while
solitary sexuality can be as rich as the imagination allows.
And since the object of the game has been redefined from
the achievement of an ethereal union of souls to a mere
physical orgasm, the presence of another person, though it
may enhance or detract from the experience, is no longer
essential.

If food is to the nineties what sex was to the fifties, that
may be a reflection of an essential difference in the two eras
in what it means to be a self. Sex is our most intimate and
defining connection to other people, and eating is our most
intimate and defining relationship to ourselves.

Why all this guilt? At other times one could explain a
guilt-ridden society in terms of a powerful church, able to
extend its reach into the souls of its faithful through the
instrument of the confessional and the threat of eternal

damnation. In the Victorian era, one could account for the hyperactive superegos that Freud encountered on his Viennese couch in terms of the repressive social practices of the day, the obsession with sexuality.

One oddity about the rise of food-related guilt is that it comes at a time when in every other domain, morality's dominion is being challenged. In the seventies there was a thriving market in workshops and seminars designed to teach us how to "get rid of the shoulds"—to turn off those nagging little voices in the back of our minds. In effect the gurus of guilt-free living were proclaiming that the old social contract was no longer valid, that the mental programming that embedded a degree of selflessness and altruism in all of us was not functional in a society no longer able to reciprocate.

That programming prepared us for a world that no longer existed by the seventies. In its place there emerged a new morality, which M. P. Baumgartner has characterized as "moral minimalism," describing it as the natural outgrowth of America's move to the suburbs. The hallmark of moral minimalism is avoidance: Rather than resolve conflicts through aggression, or through the coercive intervention of a legal apparatus, citizens of the suburbs are most inclined to avoid confrontation. "Moral minimalism is most extensive where social interaction is most diffuse. Social density breeds social control; where the first is lowest, so is the second."[4]

Baumgartner continues:

> Suburbia is growing at a rapid rate. As this happens, it appears that more and more people live in an environment characterized by transiency and fragmentation of social networks, along with spacial separation, privacy, and insulation from strangers. Increasingly, people move about freely, families scatter, and indi-

viduals are on their own, able to withdraw from others at will, without either the support or the constraints that strong social ties entail. If all this continues, moral minimalism should become an ever more pervasive feature of modern life. Suburbia may thus provide a study in the moral order of the future.[5]

One of the characteristics of suburban living that makes moral minimalism a viable solution is that residents of the suburbs don't need to get along with each other; their lives are structured in a way that maximizes their self-sufficiency. Most Americans now live in suburbs, so it is not surprising to find that the ethos that evolved in that setting has become dominant in the culture as a whole.

If the language of morality is the language with which you negotiate conflicts with your neighbor, and your way of life offers few occasions for conflict with your neighbor, then the use and usefulness of moral language is likely to be minimal.

Depending on your point of view, this can be seen either as evidence of moral progress, a sign that we are evolving a more rational and human set of societal values, or as evidence of moral decline. Social conservatives, such as Gertrude Himmelfarb and William Bennett, take the latter view, calling for a return to "traditional family values."

Himmelfarb cites with approval Margaret Thatcher's recitation of the traditional family values on which she was raised:

We were taught to work jolly hard. We were taught to prove yourself; we were taught self-reliance; we were taught to live within our income. You were taught that cleanliness is next to godliness. You were taught self-respect. You were taught always to

give a hand to your neighbour. You were taught
tremendous pride in your country. All of these
things are Victorian values. They are also perennial
values.[6]

As we have seen, they are also the values put forth in
Pinocchio. Only when Pinocchio risks his own life to save
Gepetto's does the Blue Fairy turn him into a real boy.

It's an artfully told morality tale, but it has aquired an
ironic twist over the fifty-odd years since the film's release,
given that today the Disney empire owns a worldwide network of Pleasure Islands. Only in Disneyland is it true that
"When you wish upon a star . . . anything your heart desires
will come to you." Few figures in our recent history have
played a larger role in steering our cultural shift from
Gepetto's producer ethic to the values of the consumer
ethic than Uncle Walt himself.

Those virtues have been largely abandoned in the present era, says Himmelfarb, as "morality became so thor-
oughly relativized and subjectified that virtues ceased to be
'virtues' and became 'values.'" This transformation was
achieved, in Himmelfarb's account, almost singlehandedly
by Friedrich Nietzsche, when he started using the word
"value" in a new way—to connote the moral beliefs and
attitudes of a society. It was Nietzsche's unwitting after-the-
fact accomplice, Max Weber, who popularized the term,
which was then "absorbed unconsciously and without
resistance into the ethos of modern society," leading, ultimately, to the collapse of traditional moral standards, and a
sharp rise in the rates of murder, violent crime, and illegiti-
mate births.[7]

The idea that a single philosopher could have engineered
the transformation of the moral system of the Western world
seems somewhat implausible, but Himmelfarb is surely right

about this much: We do live in a de-moralized society. The moral vocabulary no longer circulates the way it once did.

The specter of Humpty Dumpty haunts our era. There is a widespread sense that the common morality that once regulated our lives has broken into a million pieces, and that all the king's horses and all the king's men will never manage to put it together again. Deep in their hearts, all the proponents and all the opponents of "family values" know that there is no going back.

Morality is at some profound level a belief system. And what makes the return to Victorian morality, or traditional family values, or communitarianism an impossible dream is that we are no longer believers. We are aware of each of these belief systems as a such, but we no longer stand inside any one of them. All that we have left to believe in is doubt. We exist in a culture in which a multitude of belief systems coexist, and the key to coexistence is that we must respect all of them. But to do so undermines the claim of any of them to ultimate authority; we recognize them instead as social constructions.

Moral language has become like the language of another country. Young people speak it awkwardly; they know a few phrases but not the rules of grammar. It is a language that is very well suited to some particular purposes—such as negotiating the complexities of mutual obligation. But as our relationships are redefined, and our webs of mutual obligation are increasingly frayed, the language falls into disuse.

Philosophers use apocalyptic imagery to describe the current state of moral discourse. In *After Virtue,* Alasdair MacIntyre compares it to what scientific discourse would sound like in the aftermath of a cataclysm that killed all the scientists and destroyed all their texts: A few words and phrases might remain, but nobody would really know how they fit together. The title of Jeffrey Stout's *Ethics After Babel* captures the same sense of incoherence: We are all speaking different moral languages, and no one has a commanding claim to moral authority.[8]

Different theories are offered to explain the incoherence of public discourse about morals; sociologist Joshua Meyrowitz argues that the electronic media have created moral chaos by breaking down the walls that once separated coherent and homogeneous moral communities.

The grip of morality is felt most strongly in a homogeneous community, where everyone shares the same moral values, and where those who don't are clearly labeled as aberrant. An old joke captures the dilemma. As Saint Peter leads the latest arrival down the hallways of Paradise, looking for an empty room for the new guest, he suddenly becomes silent and tiptoes as he passes the door to the room that houses all the Catholics (or Protestants or Jews, in other variants of the joke.) "Shh," he says. "They think they are the only ones here."

Today it is impossible to believe that your spiritual community is the only one here. Rather, a great number of moral traditions exist side by side, offering the consumer a sort of marketplace of values. If your own spiritual tradition does not allow divorce, or the consumption of pork, or requires ascetic practices that you find onerous, shop around.

Psychologists have carved out as their own much of morality's former territory, replacing the language of morality with the language of mental health and psychopathology. The drunkard, an object of moral condemnation in the nineteenth century, has been replaced by the alcoholic, understood to be the victim of a disease.

Psychologist Stanton Peele, author of *The Diseasing of America: Addiction Treatment Out of Control,*" has argued that "the selling of the idea of addiction is a major contributor to the undermining of moral values and behavior in our era."[9]

"The problem with the therapist being cast in the moral role of teacher, of course, is that therapists have done their best to stay out of the morality business," says psychotherapist William J. Doherty. "A cornerstone of all the mainstream models of psychotherapy since Freud has been the substitution of scientific and clinical ideas for moral ideas."[10]

There are an estimated 20 million or more alcoholics (including recovering alcoholics) in the United States, and millions more Americans who have other chemical dependencies. Estimates of the number of Americans suffering from eating disorders and food addictions range as high as 80 million. Gambling addiction is also a growing category: According to the National Council on Compulsive Gamblers there are 20 million addicted gamblers.

Another addiction that gained popularity in the eighties is codependency, a loosely defined disorder originally ascribed to people who live with alcoholics; at least 40 million Americans are estimated to be codependent. The term is now more broadly applied to people who are pathologically emotionally dependent on another person or persons: As much as 95 percent of the U.S. population is said to fall into this category. Multiple addictions are common. One addiction expert has claimed that 131 million Americans are involved in some form of addictive behavior.

The disease model of addiction, originally developed to treat alcoholism, has now been extended by the addiction industry to cover codependency, compulsive gambling, sexual compulsivity, and compulsive eating. But critics of the addiction industry such as alcoholism consultant Herbert Fingarette, author of *Heavy Drinking: The Myth of Alcoholism as a Disease*, maintain that compulsive eating, gambling, and similar behaviors are not diseases, and that labeling them as such is bad science, bad medicine, and bad public policy.

The claim that alcoholism is a disease has gained widespread acceptance among the general public, but according to

Fingarette, it has little credibility among scientists. If there is such a gene, it is only one factor in a complex causal picture.

"People search around for a disease they can get behind," says Peele:

> The marketing of the disease idea, particularly the National Council on Alcoholism's selling of the idea that alcoholism is a disease, has contributed to this. And once you call alcoholism a disease, you can't stop. First compulsive gambling, then compulsive eating, then just everything, because they all follow the same patterns.[11]

There are a variety of reasons for this transformation. One is that the vocabulary of morality rests on a framework of beliefs about human nature that have largely been abandoned: Virtues, at least traditionally, are qualities of the soul, and, to make a long and complicated story short, we no longer believe in the soul.

GUILT, THE OLD MORALITY

But rather than wonder what has happened to morality, it may be more productive to inquire into the apparatus that kept it in circulation and the premises on which it operated.

We can talk about the values of a society as a set of abstract principles that can be written down as propositions. But the real power of a moral system consists of its manifestations in daily life. At the risk of seeming trendy, we may borrow a helpful term from the French and speak of the "discourse of morality." By "discourse" we mean a conversation, understood in the broadest sense.

The values of the Victorians were kept aloft through the constant circulation of this discourse, which embedded its values into family conversation and Boy Scout manuals, pronounced them from the pulpits in Sunday sermons,

carved them onto facades of public buildings, and embroi-
dered them onto pillow cases and into the plots of popular
novels. They provided a measuring stick for judging individual character.

They were also kept alive at the dinner table, where the
same morality of delayed gratification was inculcated into
children and ritualized in the order of the meal, in traditions
that survived long after the decline of Victorian sexual
mores. If you ate your peas and carrots, then you would be
rewarded with dessert—your just dessert. Moreover,
whether or not you ate your peas and carrots was not
simply a matter of personal choice; children were reminded
that there were children starving in India, and that it would
therefore be (though the logic was never completely clear)
immoral not to eat them.

The fundamental precepts of Victorian morality were
not only kept alive through circulation in the public world
but were also internalized in the conscience. To go against
that moral code would result in tremendous feelings of
remorse. There was a time within memory when we were
shocked by what seemed to be remorseless crimes, but they
now seem to occur with such frequency that it simply seems
a matter of fact that many people have no conscience—that
the having of a conscience is a sort of cultural artifact.

Victorian morality was one of character and virtue,
rather than one of rights and principles. Virtue-centered
morality, whose roots go back to Plato and Aristotle, rests
on a conception of the self as a sort of spiritual substance,
molded by education and experience into a form called
character. Character education thus became one of the central projects of Victorian morality.

But this romantic vision of the self, which was dominant
in Victorian society, was largely replaced by the modern
conception of the self, rooted in science. In this view the self
came to be essentially understood as a biological machine,

and the grand project of behavioral science became that of replacing all appeals to internal mechanisms with behavioristic explanations. The collapse of traditional morality is in part a consequence of the collapse of the traditional model of the self on which it is based. The vision of the self as having interiority has been replaced by the modernist vision of human beings as complex biological machines.

This wasn't simply a matter of scientists replacing an obsolete vocabulary with a more objective one; therapists actually often saw themselves as undoing the harm done by an excessively moralistic upbringing.

For a time guilt was being treated as the emotional equivalent of the appendix—an appendage of no known positive benefit, but with a tremendous potential to cause trouble. Psychotherapists and self-improvement experts of various stripes wrote books and offered therapies teaching people how to rid themselves of the troublesome little organ.

When we look back, part of what went on in the seventies appears to have been a language shift. In the old days the vocabulary for telling people how to lead good lives was moral and religious, including such terms as "good" and "bad," "right" and "wrong." Along came the psychologists, some of whom had a different way of seeing the world, and a completely different way of talking about it. They preferred to talk about what was healthy and unhealthy or appropriate and inappropriate. Because psychology was supposed to be scientific, and science is supposed to be objective, there was no place in their worldview for value judgments.

For a while, in fact, it became fashionable to shoot down any attempt to speak in terms of right and wrong or good and bad. Talk about morality would be countered by the question, "Isn't that a value judgment?"—usually delivered with at least the suggestion of a sneer. The implication was that value judgments were totally subjective, and therefore totally irrelevant.

People who said these sorts of things often seemed not to recognize that they had also embraced a value system, and such that such terms as "healthy" and "inappropriate"' were as value-laden as the terms they replaced.

Morality itself is an instrument, and an expression of, a social world. It only works when a certain part of each of us belongs to the larger social group. In an extremely individualistic society, the vocabulary of morality no longer makes sense.

Much of the territory once covered by morality has now been usurped. The language of law and contracts now defines relationships in the workplace, and the language of psychology and mental health is used to negotiate more intimate human interactions. Some of the words of this vocabulary have fallen so totally into disuse that they now sound merely quaint—like "wicked." Others have taken on new meanings: a sinful dessert.

The morality most of us—to varying degrees, and with significant variations in content—internalized as children was in essence the language of a social contract. These rules became the content of our consciences, that little piece of ourselves that belonged to the larger community of which we were all a part. The morality was based on the presumption that everyone else not only should but would abide by these rules as well.

The terms of this vocabulary have fallen into disuse because the underlying relationships in which they were useful are vanishing. Chastity became an important virtue because it was a key component of a social apparatus designed to regulate the production of children, and to assure that children born into a community would have persons responsible for their support. But the internalized mechanisms that made the concept of chastity work have been replaced by legal ones, and the development of more reliable methods of birth control has removed a good deal of society's interest in regulating sexual activity.

The model of human nature that saw humans as autonomous moral agents was challenged, and ultimately supplanted, by the scientific view, which saw humans from within the deterministic framework of science. Some aspects of human nature may be the result of nature, others of nurture, but all were attributable to causes that lay beyond the control of the individual.

Various factors contributed to the undermining of traditional moral values: Rather than a sudden collapse there was a gradual undermining, which can be seen as having taken place at various levels: In part the underlying cosmology was eventually abandoned. Our view of what the world, and the human self, are made of, changed. Then, as the traditional theological belief in the existence of an immortal soul gave way to the rise of the scientific worldview, the conceptual underpinnings of our moral values were weakened.

There was also a deliberate assault on some of the values— those that stood in the way of economic development. Thus frugality, a traditional Victorian value, stood in the way of economic growth, and has been under relentless assault by manufacturers, retailers, and bankers. As motivational researcher Ernst Dichter told a group of manufacturers in the fifties:

> We are now confronted with the problem of permitting the average American to feel moral ... even when he is spending, even when he is not saving, even when he is taking two vacations a year and buying a second or third car. One of the basic problems of prosperity, then, is to demonstrate that the hedonistic approach to life is a moral, not an immoral one.[12]

Increasingly the answer to the old question What will the neighbors think? is, Who cares what the neighbors think? We no longer know very many of our neighbors, nor do we talk to them, and we don't spend much time worrying about what they say to one another. Moreover, we are much more inclined than formerly to say that, whatever the subject at hand, it's none of their damned business, and usually they are likely to feel the same way.

THE NEW MORALITY

Traditionally the purpose of moral discourse has been essentially social: It inculcates in the individual those values that are most needed to preserve the social order and the viability of the social organism. These values may only indirectly benefit the individual, or in some cases may require great sacrifice of him or her.

But today the social world lies in ruins. Insofar as we have a shared world in common with our neighbors, it is the reality presented to us by the media, and insofar as we have shared values, they are those inherent in the image world. In the absence of socially articulated webs of value, the individual must turn to that world for lessons on how to construct and present a self.

It is from this encounter of the individual with the world of images that a new morality is emerging. There is a widely shared belief that we live in a world that is not only postmodern but postmoral. Against this notion I want to suggest that in fact a common morality prevails, coherent and powerful, hidden in plain view. We have absorbed a different ethic, centered on the body and the image. *Cogito ergo sum* was fine in an era of inwardness, but for the material girl or guy it is being seen and being acknowledged that constitute our reassurance that we exist. In a world of strangers, it is the surfaces that matter.

What has emerged is a harsh new morality of the body.

We don't easily recognize it as a morality because it is not articulated in the language to which we are accustomed. It is in fact a very inarticulate morality, visual rather than verbal, emerging from a new culture in which the visual predominates. The ideal is a visual one, and the ultimate good is to aspire to the physical perfection projected by it. Women strive to embody this perfection, men to possess it or control it.

The self-flagellation of medieval penitents is the closest analogy to the constant self-criticism that makes up a great part of the internal dialogue of many American women, and increasingly, men as well. The idea of the immortal soul was invented, Foucault has suggested, as a way to give the church control over the faithful. The threat that pain could be inflicted on the soul in eternity, beyond any capability of the church to inflict suffering in the temporal world, gave the church powerful leverage over the conduct of the faithful. And traditional morality has always been premised on the idea of an interior entity on which the consequences of misconduct would ultimately be visited, whether by eternal damnation or the sharp pangs of conscience in this life.

That internal entity still exists, but its moral agenda is now centered on the body. One of the most striking differences between the Magic World and our own is the near-total absence of fat people, except as occasional figures of ridicule or as villains. The meaning of this symbolic obliteration is pretty transparent: Fat people don't get into heaven.

Thus the morality of the body is not only a morality but also a religion, promising salvation to those who believe. The new cathedrals and churches are malls and fitness centers, and the new confessors are Weight Watchers counselors.

The collapse of the modernist project is also the collapse of the rationalist morality, in which the principles of morality could somehow be deduced from commonly accepted ideas about human happiness and utility. In this

harsh new morality, fat is bad. One very common explanation of why fatness is stigmatized is that fatness is the outer
sign of an inner weakness: If you are fat, it is a sign that you
lack self-control.

But that morality is really obsolete. In the new morality,
in which appearance is paramount, fat is bad *because* it is
bad. A lack of self-control is bad only because it might result
in fatness. But if you can manage to stay slender without self-
control, so much the better for you: A large new segment of
the food market is built around the promise of self-indulgence without consequences. And alternately, if you are
obese in spite of great self-control, too bad for you: One of
the fundamental tenets of this morality is that life isn't fair.

Because appetite is insatiable, the struggle is endless.
"Eat what you like," urges an advertisement for Healthy
Choice luncheon meats. But the reader knows that he or she
can't eat what he or she likes, at least when it comes to luncheon meats. And so Healthy Choice holds out the promise
of pleasure without sin, in the form of 97 percent fat-free luncheon meats. "I forget," says the model in the ad. "What am I
giving up again?"

The new moral imperative is, in the words of the U.S.
Army recruiting slogan, to "be all that you can be." And the
image of what it is that we may become is that projected by
advertising and the mass media. We could have perfect
bodies, if we were only more disciplined about eating and
exercise, and we could own nicer cars and bigger houses if
we worked harder or worked smarter. These things are not
merely desirable in themselves or because of the eroticism
invested in them by advertising; they are also carriers of
moral value, our proof that we are trying hard to be all that
we can be. But the task grows ever more challenging as the
possibilities of our consumer culture expand our options. It
is now possible to choose not to be bald, by choosing hair
transplants or monoxidil.

In a reality brought to us by sponsors, it is hardly a surprise that buying becomes the ultimate good. Since consuming, rather than eating, is the object of the game, an enormous amount of energy has gone into developing forms of food and drink that allow one to consume without being fulfilled: diet food and drink, beverages free of alcohol or caffeine. Not far away are a new generation of foods whose molecular structure lets them pass through the body entirely undigested.

It would be a mistake to view this new morality of the body in strictly negative terms. Rather, it defines a field of play in which the individual can articulate a sense of self, by engaging in moral battles and making moral choices. It is this moral dimension that gives consumerism meaning; there may ultimately be little satisfaction in all the toys that we acquire over a lifetime, but the toys are a sign of our success, our inward grace.

The Gospel According to Weight Watchers

It's the weight loss industry's ugly little secret: Diets don't work. But even if diets don't help people lose weight, they do offer a solution to another challenge of modern life: the hunger for structure and meaning.

Trouble is, it's a bad solution.

AS AMERICAN AS DIET COLA

Dieting has become a way of life for millions of Americans. Diet foods, once a specialty-food category largely reserved for diabetics, have entered the mainstream. Combined sales of Diet Coke and Diet Pepsi now exceed one billion dollars per year, and reduced-calorie prepared entrees such as Lean Cuisine, Weight Watchers, and Healthy Choice have captured a large share of the frozen-entree market.

Fast food has become diet food too; as low fat became the hot food trend of the nineties, chains like McDonald's rushed to market their versions—McLean Deluxe Burger, Hardee's Real Lean Deluxe burger, and KFC's Lite 'n' Crispy skinless fried chicken. All told, Americans spend some forty-seven billion dollars per year on the diet and exercise industry.

The increased consumption of low-fat foods does not mean that Americans are consuming fewer calories. Rather, the lower calorie count means that we can eat more by volume. The famous "great taste, less filling" Miller Lite commercials of the 1980s promised just that—you could consume more, because these beers wouldn't fill you up. Eating has been disconnected from physical hunger and connected to the emotional and psychological needs of the consumer.

NEVER SAY DIET

You can call them food plans, or you can call them eating plans, says the weight-loss industry, but please don't call them diets. The word "diet" is taboo now that the message has finally gotten out that diets don't work. According to Diane Epstein and Kathleen Thompson, authors of *Feeding on Dreams: Why America's Diet Industry Doesn't Work—And What Will Work for You*, only one out of five diet-program clients loses any weight at all. Of those clients who do lose weight, only one out of ten keeps the weight off for two years, and only one out of fifty keeps the weight off for seven years. The rest gain back any weight they lose, and typically start the cycle all over again.

Diets don't work because the body, sooner or later, rebels against them. According to one popular but controversial theory, diets are actually counterproductive, because the body adapts to the reduced-calorie intake by burning fat more efficiently. When the diet ends, and the dieter returns to a prediet level of consumption, the body's now-more-efficient metabolic machinery is able to store as fat more of the calories consumed.

If it seems puzzling that the diet industry continues to grow despite its failure to cure obesity, it is equally puzzling that obesity continues to grow despite the billions spent on diet books, foods, soft drinks, stays at weight-loss clinics, and other nostrums.

The sedentary lifestyles of many Americans are often cited as a contributory cause of obesity, but all other things being equal, a reduction in activity should translate into a reduction in appetite and calorie consumption, not greater consumption and more obesity.

In virtually any other line of business, such poor rates of success would spell disaster, but in the diet industry they are the key to success. Most of the business—estimates run as high as 90 percent—at diet centers is repeat business. A diet that really worked would cut a swath of devastation through the industry like the legendary ten-year light bulb.

DIETING AS A WAY OF LIFE

While advertising and the mass media project a vision of the promised land, the diet and exercise industries promise us the means to get there. Although nearly every consumer product, from wristwatches to automobiles, is marketed with some implicit or explicit message about how the product will help us become the kind of person we want to be—or at least to project the kind of image that we want to project—the diet and exercise industries speak to us in a particularly powerful way because they address our relationship to our bodies. Using positive language in their relentlessly upbeat commercials and brochures—language that contrasts with the negative self-images to which they speak—they offer the hope of redemption to all who carry around their body hatred as a secret burden.

Diets are hardly new, and neither is the use of physical

and medical treatments to shape the body to the contours currently in vogue. What is new is the degree to which diet consciousness has penetrated the culture, and the kind of self that responds to the barrage of messages about body image and weight loss. Rather than a cure, weight watching has become a way of life.

It is a struggle that is painful and almost always unsuccessful, and yet the struggle gives meaning, order, and organization to dieters' lives. In a world in which all values are relative, this one seems an absolute: Thin is better than fat; firm is better than flabby. And in a world in which so much seems out of our individual control, whether we are fat or thin at least is something that, theoretically, we should be able to control. Gaining this control offers a meaningful template for self-invention.

We all have a fundamental need for our lives to be about something, and in each era and each culture, this something takes a different form. In an era when the church reigned supreme in people's lives, it was about seeking salvation. The calculus of mortal sins and venial sins, penances and indulgences, may have been a powerful mechanism for giving the church control over the conduct of the faithful, but it also gave the faithful a way of making sense out of the universe. Today it is the diet, in its infinite variations, that provides the faithful with a moral playground.

Dieting is the new religion; it projects a vision of the person you can strive to become, offers symbols of good and evil, a daily ritual to achieve, and even, in the form of the Weight Watchers weigh-in, a confessional. And eating is the new sin. With every bite you take, you move farther away from the perfection that you must achieve in order to enter the kingdom of heaven. And so the thrust of a great deal of food advertising is the selling of indulgences—the promise of foods that offer the pleasure of indulgence without the price.

DIETING YOUR WAY TO THE NEW YOU

The advertising pitches of the diet and exercise industries don't simply promise to help you lose weight; rather, they promise to help you become a new you. Jenny Craig's Personal Weight Management Profile encourages prospective customers to create a vision of their future by spelling out on a worksheet what they will be able to do once they lose weight. "What sort of clothes will you be able to wear that you cannot wear now? What activities will be easier to participate in? How will your relationships with other people change? How will living this new lifestyle make you feel about yourself?"

Although this copy suggests that weight loss occurs within a finite period of time, for dieters, the journey is never over. At Jenny Craig, where some 90 percent of revenues come from sales of Jenny's Cuisine, clients are strongly encouraged to eat only the company's packaged products, although after the first four or five weeks, they are permitted to substitute meals from a Jenny Craig cookbook. As one industry analyst explains it, "Jenny Craig wants customers to view weight-loss programs as they view a trip to the beauty salon—as a consumer service, to be used when needed."[1] It is no different at rival Weight Watchers, where clients are encouraged to become lifetime members, and to sign up for the Personal Cuisine plan, "a complete program of delicious, pre-packaged, portion-controlled breakfasts, lunches, dinners, and snacks," available only to members.

The new culture of addictions lies at the heart of Richard Simmons's Deal-A-Meal Weight Loss Progam, but so does the old morality of self-denial. Each Deal-A-Meal Kit includes menu cards, instructional video, and a Deal-A-Meal wallet, to be stuffed with colored cards (red for protein, pink for fruit) that you can "spend" each day. Simmons, best known for his *Sweating with the Oldies* exercise videos, offers an approach to dieting that conflates eating, spending, and Alcoholics Anonymous–style spirituality.

"I admit that *I love food* and I am *addicted* to it," is the first point in Simmons's twenty-point program, clearly inspired by the famous twelve steps of Alcoholics Anonymous. There is no mention here, though, of a higher power; it is the dieter's own willpower that must save her. But that's a lot to hope for; the implication here is that food addiction, like alcoholism, it is a lifelong affliction. As millions of dieters know all to well, a relapse can set in at any moment.

The key, according to point three of the program, is to take responsibility: "I have blamed many people and many things for my fat, but I must admit *I am to blame.* I hold the fork." And a dose of positive thinking helps as well, as point sixteen makes clear: "I am a terrific person and I like myself right now, no matter what I weigh." But ultimately, it comes down to willpower: "The next time I have a *craving* for anything I know is fattening or am tempted not to exercise, I will think about the *new me*, and I will be strong."

Simmons asks his dieters not only to practice abstinence but also asks them to sweat—although his *Sweating with the Oldies* tapes try hard to make aerobic exercise seem like fun. That's asking a lot these days. If dieting was difficult in the age when the way to heaven was to resist the temptations of the flesh, today it is all but impossible, for consuming is an integral part of our identities.

Weight Watchers promises an easier path to thinness. The June edition of *Weight Watchers Extra* comes addressed to Current Resident. It is an advertising brochure for Weight Watchers, packaged as a magazine, and the bold headlines on the cover don't simply describe the stories inside; they also promise wonderful changes in the life of C. Resident. MAKEOVER MAGIC promises one headline. "IT'S NOT TOO LATE . . . to Get In Shape for Summer" promises the next—even though it is already June. And a third invites the reader to "TRY OUR BACON CHEESEBURGER! You're Sure to Gobble It Up!"

You may think that gobbling is what got you into this predicament to begin with, but Weight Watchers promises that you can have your bacon cheeseburger and eat it too. The bacon cheeseburger, for which a recipe is featured on page 16, isn't actually the juicy greasy slider that torments dieters' dreams; it's a simulation of a cheeseburger, made from two and a half ounces of ground turkey, a strip of turkey bacon, and less than an ounce of Monterey Jack. It's permissible for weight watchers because it lacks most of the fat that makes real cheeseburgers taste so good. Timely, too, since June is also Turkey Lover's Month.

The svelte model on the cover, posing next to a photograph of her fat former self, is identified inside as Barbara Cross, Weight Watchers 1993 International Member of the Year, who has maintained her seventy-pound weight loss for the past five years. She is living proof that makeover magic is possible, and that no matter how overweight you may be, you can still get in shape for summer.

If you're still hungry, there's lot more to eat in the pages of *Weight Watchers Extra*—a root-beer float, made with diet root beer and frozen vanilla low-fat dairy dessert (June is also Dairy Month) and mouthwatering photographs of Weight Watchers Breakfast-On-The-Go! blueberry muffins and a Chocolate Chip Cookie Dough Sundae from Weight Watchers Sweet Celebrations line of Frozen Desserts.

The best treats, though, are reserved for people who join Weight Watchers. If you join by July 1, you get a coupon book with more than $230 in terrific discounts, including savings on Hertz car rentals and JCPenney photography, and best of all, a buy-one-get-one-free offer for a gooey cheesy pizza from Little Caesars. (These are Baby Pan! Pan! pizzas—the kind you can eat by yourself. As for the free pizza, you can take it home and keep it in the refrigerator in case you feel like a snack later on.)

Joining also makes you eligible to buy Weight Watchers

Personal Cuisine, a complete prepackaged portion-controlled food plan featuring such gourmet fare as Burgundy Wine Sauce with Beef Sirloin Tips & Seasoned Fettucine Noodles, or even Personal Cuisine Black Forest Cake à la Mode for a snack. That's just one of the three food plans that Weight Watchers currently offers; the others are the Fat & Fiber Plan and the Improved Selection Plan.

But like Jenny Craig, what Weight Watchers is really selling is a new self-image. "You are Extra Special!" the magazine announces in large type. In fact, every Current Resident is extra special:

> Losing a few pounds can be the *first* step toward improving your image. But in order to really make positive changes in your life, you need to feel good about yourself.
>
> Start by focusing on your qualities. Are you honest, loving, full of fun? Do you reach out warmly to people?
>
> Then consider your talents. It's not important to be a great athlete or a terrific singer; what really matters are things that make a difference to those around you.
>
> Most important of all, take time to appreciate the beautiful things about your body: Your expressive eyes, your graceful hands, your physical strength.
>
> Remember—losing weight can be much easier if you first discover just how special you are.

The copywriting invokes the familiar vocabulary of positive thinking. But the implied metaphysics embedded in this text is one in which the highest reality is that of the image, the projected shadows that we produce in the consciousnesses of others.

DIETING AND THE NEW SELF

The rates of failure of weight-loss programs are so high as to demand an explanation. What is wrong with us that we can't resist, even for a few weeks or a day, the temptation of a chocolate dessert? We make resolutions, and by nightfall they are broken—we surrender, most often, without a fight.

One explanation for this cycle is the postwar emergence of a different kind of self. In the nineteenth century over-eating had moral significance for Sylvester Graham and his followers; it was the sin of gluttony, and the moral duty was to resist it lest the soul be corrupted. The Protestant work ethic that fueled the development of capitalism was at its heart a producer ethic. To be strong, one had to deny and delay one's gratifications. The cure was abstinence.

Today the identity that we seek to project is one that can only be articulated through what we posess or consume; abstinence is out of the question. (Moreover, abstinence resists commodification.) In this culture, the only possible cure for too much consumption is more consumption. Weight Watchers does not ask you to give up anything, but rather invites you to eat your way to your ideal weight.

You don't really have to give anything up, the advertising promises; you can even have a bacon cheeseburger. But in actuality you can't have a bacon cheeseburger, only a simulacrum of one. Your body isn't fooled for long; almost invariably it rebels. Sooner or later your vigilance slips, and you have consumed a real bacon cheeseburger.

Weight Watchers' encouraging customers to gobble their way to slenderness captures perfectly an internal contradiction within our economy that ultimately manifests itself in contradictory behaviors. As feminist philosopher Susan Bordo expresses it:

On the one hand, as producers of goods and services we must sublimate, delay, repress desires for
immediate gratification; we must cultivate the work
ethic. On the other hand, as consumers we must display a boundless capacity to capitulate to desire and
indulge in impulse; we must hunger for constant and
immediate satisfaction. The regulation of desire thus
becomes an ongoing problem, as we find ourselves
endlessly besieged by temptation, while socially
condemned for overindulgence. . . . In this way, the
central contradiction of the system inscribes itself
on our bodies, and bulimia emerges as a characteristic modern personality construction.[2]

The fifty-billion-dollar diet industry moves ever forward,
driven by a two-stroke engine. The one stroke is the insatiable
hunger of the American consumer, the other is the constant
urge to lose weight. The perfect consumer is the one who is
forever propelling the economy forward on the downstroke,
and on the upstroke, gobbling bacon cheeseburgers and then
attending Weight Watchers meetings to take off those extra
pounds.

BODY HATRED, BODY OBSESSION

The management of the body has become the central life
project of many middle-class women, and an increasing
number of men. What drives the industry is the intensive
body hatred that so many women feel. More than 75 percent
of American women "feel fat," and one out of four college-
age women is bulimic.[3] This body hatred is postmodernity's
answer to original sin. The old Christian doctrine has few
serious adherents nowadays, but a belief in their own physical inadequacy is a central and obsessive preoccupation for
most American women, regardless of their weight. Body

hatred and body monitoring have become crucial organizing principles of many people's lives.

It is ironic that this intense body hatred has become so widespread only a few decades after women in large numbers stopped wearing girdles. That liberation, it turns out, was short-lived. Instead of wearing external girdles, many women felt constrained to internalize them, to mold their bodies through exercise, into the shapes that once were achieved by artifice. And now the pendulum swings again. Girdles, in new forms, are coming back into fashion, along with control-top pantyhose and Wonder Bras.

This is an extension of the American replacement of nature. Just as the physical environment is progressively being replaced by a manufactured landscape, the territory of the body is increasingly colonized. The process of remolding bodies, and especially women's bodies, is not new, but new technologies, ranging from tummy tucks and liposuction to breast enlargements or reductions and baldness cures, extend the domain over which women, and increasingly men, are expected to exercise control. If we are fat, then, it is our failing, because it is something we could fix.

"There is, of course, nothing new in women's preoccupation with youth and beauty," says feminist philosopher Sandra Bartky.

> What is new is the extraordinary emphasis currently being given to the female appearance and the exhaustive and invasive character of the techniques required to "enhance" this appearance. New, too, is the spread of this discipline to all classes of women and its deployment throughout the life-cycle. What was formerly the specialty of the aristocrat or courtesan is now the routine obligation of every woman, be she a grandmother or a barely pubescent girl.[4]

Why have these images of women become popular in the culture, and why have they changed? Going back through American history, we can see a constant reconfiguring of women's bodies in accordance with the ideals of each age, from the whalebone-corseted women of the Victorian era to the girdled shapes of the fifties, and finally to the anorexic adolescent figure currently in vogue.

Roughly speaking, it's pretty easy to see a correlation between the role that society envisions for women in any given period, and the images that it projects. In traditional societies in which women's fertility is the key to the prosperity of the family or the community, women with large breasts and broad hips are likely to become sex symbols.

Rosie the Riveter rolled up her sleeve to display an impressive bicep in the forties, but by the fifties, when gender roles were most sharply pronounced and women were being squeezed out of the workforce into domestic roles, there was a renewed passion for women whose body type accentuated gender difference: big breasts and hips, suitable for producing the postwar baby boom.

When men began to balk at the breadwinner role, and the pill made the option of recreational sex easier, the curvacious body of the fifties was quickly replaced by the slenderer waif look, epitomized by models Twiggy and Jean Shrimpton, and, much later, Kate Moss.

Nearly all of us, to a greater or lesser degree, give space inside our heads to a little inspector general who is constantly monitoring our body shape and image. In the case of women, he tends to be more tyrannical, in the case of men, more forgiving. (Research shows that women typically overestimate their weight, while men underestimate theirs.) Far from resenting his presence or questioning his authority, many men, and more women, submit themselves blindly to his authority. This might seem like sheer cowardice, but, though trapped inside our heads, the little inspector general has ample reinforcements outside. Women, especially are constantly subject to the male gaze, which many times a day repeats the internal inspector's message.

As art critic John Berger put it: "Men look at women. Women watch themselves being looked at. This determines not only the relationship of men to women, but also the relationship of women to themselves."[5] Women look at men, too, of course, but less often and more discreetly; it is the look that men give women that conveys an instant appreciation of their standing, their desirability, their competitiveness in the beauty market.

The gaze is regulative; it is an inspection with a summary report. Fat women get a quick dismissive glance, slender women a slow undressing. It can of course be debated whether it is better to be looked at or ignored. If some looking-at is degrading, then so is not being looked at—being treated as invisible. The gaze is also objectifying; as it awards points for how well the body in question conforms to an ideal, it rewards the woman in question for her success in objectifying herself.

Another reason eating disorders are more intense for women than for men may be that women have been the principal consumers for longer. Because the earliest commodities were household goods, and because both domestic work and shopping for household goods has traditionally been women's work, women have been the targets of most of the advertising. Now, however, that is changing. The decline of the breadwinner ethic and the rise of the consumer society have given men more money to spend on themselves, and the social permission to do so.

If preoccupation with the body was traditionally a female issue, that may be because the culture reproduced a split along essentially gender lines between subjects and objects. Men have traditionally been raised to see themselves as subjects and agents, women to see themselves as objects acted upon. But this split no longer breaks nearly so cleanly along chromosomal lines. Rather, there are now strong cultural trends that defy that identification, both from females who resist objectification and from males who embrace it.

Increasingly the preoccupation with the body is becoming widespread among men as well, as men's bodies become the focus of advertising. Within an economic system that constantly requires the development of new markets, men's bodies are simply one more territory to exploit. Thus advertising sells designer underwear or men's fragrances or health club memberships, or even diet soft drinks, by inviting men to look at themselves more critically. The growing presence of magazines such as *GQ* and *Men's Health* are both causes and symptoms of this trend. As cultural critic Frank Mort has observed,

> Young men are being sold images which rupture traditional icons of masculinity. They are stimulated to look at themselves—and other men—as objects of consumer desire. They are getting pleasures previously branded taboo or feminine. A new bricollage of masculinity is the noise coming from the fashion house, the market place, and the street.[6]

RECONCILING TWO MYTHS

The person of average weight may suffer as much from eating disorders as the person who is anorexic or morbidly obese—the only difference is that instead of being caught in the grip of one compulsion, he or she is torn between two. Bordo suggests that the "ideal" consumer is bulimic, torn between the two drives.[7]

At the core of the struggle is the need to reconcile two irreconcilable myths: the one that says that if only you were slender then your life would be fulfilled, and the other that promises fulfillment through eating. Both of these myths are ultimately myths about the self; advertising promises this reconciliation: I dreamed I dieted and went to heaven.

Is there no way out of this insanity? Susan Powter says there is, and her message has propelled her to celebrity status in the diet and exercise world.

By the time Powter arrives for her scheduled book signing at the Mall of America, the line of women has grown to several hundred. Some have waited two hours or longer for the chance to get her autograph, shake her hand, and to tell her, in the brief moment that they will have face-to-face with her, how grateful they are for all that she has done for them. A few have tears in their eyes.

The aura of the appearance resembles that of a revival meeting; Powter has given these women new hope, has set them free from the bondage of diets and compulsive overeating. More precisely, what Powter has done is to tap into the pain, and the anger, of a generation of American women. Propelled to celebrity status by a successful infomercial, she has built a career around the simple message that serves as the title of her bestselling first book: *Stop the Insanity.*

"I'm not angry, damn it. I'm passionate," writes Powter, in the introduction. "Passionate about getting this message out to every woman on earth. Passionate about stopping the insanity. The insanity of starvation, deprivation, and destroying our self-esteem for the sake of skinniness. The insanity that has affected, and all too often ruined, the lives of millions of women. . . ."

On the facing page, there is a photograph of the author, wearing body-clinging tights that show the contours of lean

muscular thighs, and a sweatshirt cut off to reveal a bare
midriff and perfectly flat stomach.

Written in classic self-help style, the book is full of the
first-name-only stories that typify the genre: "Betty, who lost
the enamel on her teeth and was hospitalized with a hiatal
hernia from eating so much," and Teresa, who lost 126
pounds on a doctor-sponsored liquid-fast program, but lost
the weight so quickly that her skin was hanging from her
body.

But the most compelling story is Powter's own:

> I was a 260-pound housewife, feeling desperately out
> of control, afraid, hurting physically and emotion-
> ally, trying every diet out there and . . . failing. . . .
> Each diet I tried led to failure, and each failure led to
> the next. When one diet didn't work, I'd go right on
> to another—liquid starvation, pills, shakes, diet
> bars, or whatever was being blasted at me as the
> answer.[8]

Powter promises a way out of "the problem that faces
millions of us: hating the way you look and feel: never-
ending dieting, starvation and deprivation, those self-esteem
beatings that we live with every day of our lives."[9]

Ultimately, though, Powter's solution to body hatred is
not body acceptance, but a new way to win the game. Stop
dieting, Powter tells her followers, and start eating. Start
exercising and breathing right, and you can have the body
you want.

Powter's text doesn't say what that body should look
like; the dominant message is that that body can be whatever you want it to be, as long as you are healthy and happy.
But that message is undercut by the photograph on page
280 of *Stop the Insanity*, which shows a slender and muscular

Susan Powter in high heels and a thong bikini. "There isn't a woman in this country who doesn't want to be able to put on a thong bikini and jump up and down and not wiggle all over," says Powter.

The advice to stop dieting is hardly revolutionary; no one has embraced it more enthusiastically than the diet industry, which now avoids talk of diets in favor of talk about "lifestyle change." Instead of dieting, Powter urges, her readers and viewers should eat as much as they want, never skip a meal again, and increase their activity level.

Is there a catch? Of course there is. The devil is in the details: You can eat whatever you want as long as you avoid fat. To look like Powter, the women at the Mall of America would have to stick, for a very long time, to a regimen that burns off more calories than they consume.

To achieve her look of slender muscularity Powter herself follows a diet that is almost entirely vegetarian and exercises more than an hour a day. Setting aside the matter of the self-discipline required by such a regimen, the realities of most women's lives make it virtually impossible to keep that kind of fat-free diet, and equally difficult to find an hour—or even a half hour—every day for regular exercise. So Susan Powter is in fact offering the same solution in different clothing. Her frame of reference is the same old body hatred.

REALLY STOPPING THE INSANITY

Is there a way out of this nightmare? Feminist psychotherapists Carol Munter and Jane Hirschmann, authors of *When Women Stop Hating Their Bodies*, say that instead of trying to win the diet game, women should just stop playing:

> The time has come for us to stop torturing ourselves in ways that we would not treat any other human being," states their manifesto. "The time has

come for us to stop the dieting that has become a life-long, life-draining preoccupation. Dieting has turned millions of us into food junkies, driven compulsive eaters who grow fatter every year. The time has come for us to enjoy our bodies in all their diversity. The time has come for us to reclaim our appetites, our bodies, and our selves.[10]

Easier said than done. Women are urged to learn to distinguish between mouth hunger, which uses food as a tranquilizer, and stomach hunger, which signals real physiological needs. Instead of eating in response to the clock or feelings of stress, you learn to eat when the body signals a need for fuel and to respond to mouth hunger with appropriate emotional caretaking.

And, most important, women are encouraged to challenge the messages that they have internalized from the dominant culture about body size and beauty. "Who says that youth is more attractive than age?" the authors ask rhetorically. "Who says that fat is bad and thin is good? . . . Who says that thin is sexy?" In place of those messages readers are told to "create an internal caretaker who can provide us with what we really need—unconditional acceptance, attention and empowerment—so that food can resume its proper place in our lives."

For many women and men these prescriptions may be helpful. They are certainly a beginning. But the questions Hirschmann and Munter ask so dismissively are not so easily dismissed. "Who says that thin is sexy?" Half the magazines on the newsstand, and most of the commercials on television. When those images and messages are everywhere, an internal caretaker giving us positive messages may not be sufficient.

The needs created by the diet and exercise industries are impossible to satisfy, and in an odd way, this is what makes them so powerful. Anorexics are in the grip of one compulsion, compulsive eaters another. But it would be mistaken to assume that those who are neither anorexic nor compulsive eaters are free from either compulsion; the garden variety dieter is typically in the grip of both—where a forty-seven-billion-dollar industry depends on them to be.

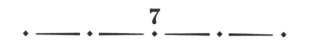

7

Making
Peace with Food

Amid all this gloomy talk about food anxieties and food disorders, it's easy to forget that eating can be, should be, and often still is one of life's greatest pleasures.

The problem for many of us is not that we take too much pleasure from food, but rather that we take too little. For all our consumption, conspicuous and otherwise, we too often find ourselves, as the philosopher Alan Watts once put it, eating the menu rather than the meal.

One starting place, then, might be to think seriously about the phenomenology of enjoyment: Though we tend to use the words somewhat interchangeably, there are important differences between "fun," "pleasure," and "joy," and the kinds of eating associated with each. Each corresponds to a different state of the self.

Fun is a momentary diversion, a little vacation from the rest of your life. Fun foods give us a fizz, jolt, snap, crackle, or pop. "The fun begins with Dole," says a current commercial, which evokes banana-peel pratfalls and reminds you that Dole bananas are full of "vitamins, minerals, and laughs."

"Be Young, Have Fun, Drink Pepsi," advises another recent slogan. Fun foods are Screaming Yellow Zonkers and Pop Rocks and Doritos.

Advertisements for fun foods and beverages tend to show people eating or drinking while having fun doing something else, like whitewater rafting or flirting at parties. Fun foods tend not to have complex flavors, and they don't need to; they stimulate us with crunch or fizz instead. Fun foods take us away from ourselves.

Sensual pleasure is a notch up in the pantheon of satisfactions. Pleasure requires more focused attention than fun. When foods taste good, the more carefully we concentrate on enjoying them and the more satisfaction we derive.

Of course, if the food doesn't really taste very good, then focusing our attention on its flavor is likely to make the eating experience less pleasurable, not more.*

Joyful eating is the highest form of eating satisfaction. "Joy" suggests the soul's well-being. Images of family feasts and celebrations come to mind. Joyful eating can be as simple as a loaf of bread and a jug of wine, but it is the presence of thou, as Omar Khayyám would have said, that makes it joyful. Often, though, the meal at joyful celebrations is more elaborate: We choose our most lavish fare to betoken the preciousness of the moment. Food has an essential role in such celebrations: It is the tangible symbol of a bond that unites us. But here the level of consumption that middle-class Americans have come to take for granted

---

* We can anticipate the objection that whether foods taste good or not is a purely subjective matter. The old Roman adage *De gustibus non disputandum est* (In matters of taste there can be no dispute) notwithstanding, in matters of taste there is actually a great deal of agreement, evidenced in everything from the scores given at wine tastings to the fact that some restaurants tend to be more popular than others and some cuts of meat more expensive than others, though taste is never the only factor.

has made it harder to preserve the meaning of feasting; even the biblical feast of the prodigal son would seem plain by comparison with the level of sumptuousness that expense account diners have come to take for granted.

What joy is about, at its heart, is a sense of connectedness, whether to another human being, a community, or the rest of creation. It is a sense that escapes us when we relate to food as subject to object, exchanging pieces of green paper for boxes with pretty pictures on them.

Many of us now reside pretty far away from that state of joyfulness. We're eating in response to an inner emptiness that food cannot satisfy, locked in a losing battle against our own bodies as we try to conform to impossible physical ideals. The same marketplace culture that surrounds us with fantasies of gastronomic ecstasy and impossible ideals of slenderness cashes in once again by selling nostrums to cure our unhappiness: weight-loss pills and psychotherapy, hard-body tapes and fat-free ice creams.

The situation is far from hopeless, however. As we have seen, every era has produced its own characteristic formation of the self, from the soulful inward-looking self of the romantic era, to the highly rational self of modern times, to the fragmented self of the current age. What distinguishes the current moment is that we have reached a new level of self-consciousness about ourselves, our diets, and the reality that we have constructed. But if that new level of self-consciousness is at the heart of many of the contemporary anxieties about eating, it may also be the key to resolving them.

Once we realize that our self-images and the meanings that we attach to food are a part of our socially constructed reality, it becomes possible consciously to change them. This era, too, shall pass, and we all have a role to play in shaping the next.

From what has been said so far, it might sound as if the only way to heal our relationship with food is to heal and repair the world. And although that may seem like a hopeless task, really the opposite is true: Food can be the concrete starting point for healing our relationship with ourselves and our planet.

But to create new possibilities, we must first have a clearer understanding of how our self-understanding is shaped by our culture, and then develop a vision of the kinds of selves we want to become. Taking ethics seriously turns out to be an essential element of this project, as does developing a more mindful relationship with food.

One tempting solution is to try to go backward in time, to re-create a coherent culture from a bygone era. Some people may still find an adequate model of personhood within an ethnic or religious tradition, and others may find it within ethical ideals from secular, modernist traditions. If that works for you, more power to you. But, at least for most of us, there can be no going back. We can only move forward. Nostalgic visions of small-town America notwithstanding, our world, our lives, and our selves are too complex to fit back into the patterns of a simpler and more innocent time.

We have taken another bite of the apple. The innocence with which we once were able to bite into a wedge of cheesecake or a slice of veal is gone forever. The world we lived in before Julia Child may not have been the Garden of Eating, but it is just as irretrievably lost.

CHANGING THE WORLD, STARTING WITH FOOD

Getting free of food anxieties and eating disorders requires thinking differently about who we are and what we value. The solution, though, is not something we'll ever be able to purchase or consume. It lies, rather, in developing a sense of who we are that resists the consumer model, and in creating a reality that sustains that vision.

Consumption isn't the only source of our identity, of course, but it is the dominant one. Our common vocabulary is the vocabulary of advertising. Our culture has evolved not only highly advanced technologies for the production of consumer goods but equally advanced technologies for the production of consumers. To keep the great engines of production operating at full capacity, we must be stimulated to consume constantly and, more fundamentally, constantly to feel the need to consume.

The fact that the values and ideology of consumerism are so deeply embedded in our social reality means that strategies to escape that focus on the individual alone aren't likely to be very successful. It is extremely difficult to decide, for example, that from this moment forward body size will have a different meaning for me than it does for the society as a whole. This is not only because the society is saturated with messages about body size, or because anyone who resists the prevailing attitude is likely to pay a social penalty. Ultimately it is because even when those obstacles are overcome, the greatest obstacle is inscribed in our own hearts: We ourselves have bought into those cultural messages.

Of course this example is oversimplified. "We" *don't* all feel the same way about body size. There are spaces within the culture where fatness is considered beautiful, or else is treated simply as a matter of indifference. And it is the existence of those "free zones," as embattled or imperfect as they may be, that points to the possibility of resistance, and even liberation.

Even when we recognize our own prejudices, as the experience of racism shows, it can be enormously difficult to root them out. We reach yet another difficulty, though, when our problems are so deeply embedded that we don't even perceive that they exist. Thus, even though our ultimate goal, if we are to escape the eater's dilemma, must be to create a different kind of world, or at least a space within this one where a different reality prevails, our starting point must be to bring to consciousness some of the elements of our way of looking at the world that we have more or less taken for granted.

If the idea of creating a different reality sounds a little too cosmic, let's bring it down to earth. Our current version of reality—the consumer society—is a relatively recent invention. Though a small class of Americans was able to support a consumer lifestyle as far back as the late nineteenth century, the mass consumer society as we know it today didn't really come into existence until after World War II.

It is part of the consumer dynamic that the great engines of manufacture and marketing continually must chew up more and more of our landscape, physical and emotional, and convert it into goods to be consumed, whether as food products or experiences. What makes it so difficult is that our very sense of who we are is tied up with our role as consumers. This craving for more makes us a little like vampires, ever on the prowl for fresh blood. Insofar as it's possible, one way to start is by trying to turn off the little voice that tells us we must acquire and acquire again.

OPTING OUT OF CONSUMERISM

What would it mean to not be a consumer? At first glance it might seem that the only way to stop being a consumer would be to stop eating. But even though consuming and eating have become virtually synonymous, there are important distinctions to be made between consuming as a biological process and consuming as a way of life. "In almost all its early English uses," writes British literary critic Raymond Williams, "*consume* had an unfavorable sense; it meant to destroy, to use up, to waste, to exhaust."[1] When our ancestors came to this country, most of them came as farmers, accustomed to a way of life in which it was vitally important not to use up, waste, or exhaust. To produce their daily bread they had to exercise careful stewardship, taking care of their land year after year so that it would take care of them.

Opting out of consumerism doesn't mean not eating, and it doesn't even necessarily mean not owning things. Rather, it means developing a relationship with the stuff we use in this world that goes beyond engulfing and devouring. The key is to reenchant the world, to expand our concept of ourselves in such a way that we experience our interbeing, as the Vietnamese Buddhist monk, teacher, and peace activist Thich Nhat Hanh would say. There is much we can do within the parameters of our current roles as consumers, both to redefine the meaning of food in our lives, and to make our choices as consumers express our values.

THE LOGIC OF I-IT

It is part of the tragedy of the bounded empty self that it seeks to connect but can only consume. The object of desire literally disappears, but the sense of connection is never achieved. This is the relationship that Martin Buber characterized as I-It. When Buber spoke of the I-It relationship as a way of being in the world that radically separates subject and object, he contrasted it with another way of being that he called I-Thou. The I of the I-Thou is fundamentally in relationship, fundamentally inseparable from the world of its concerns.

We have taken the logic of I-It about as far as it can go. It has given us a mastery over the physical world that our ancestors could hardly have imagined. The logic of I-It enables us to take everything in the world apart, break it down into smaller and smaller pieces, and reassemble it to our liking. But it is precisely this mastery that alienates us from the world.

One of the elements of the modernist perspective that we must be prepared to let go of is its thoroughgoing materialism. "There is absolutely no difference," scientists assure us, "between a glass of organic milk and a glass of milk produced with bovine growth hormone." But the difference isn't one that scientists will ever be able to detect in their laboratories.

The difference is the story that comes attached to each. The milk may be chemically the same, but everything else is different: the life of the farmer who produced the milk, the amount of suffering inflicted on the cow, the health of the larger community of which the dairy farm is a part. One myth of the modern era is that we can chop the world into parts so small that the stories disappear. But what we find is that we cannot live without them. These stories nourish us just as the food itself.

The mass-marketers understand our hunger for these stories, and so they package their products with stories: stories about men and women who find romance over a cup of instant coffee, or busy fathers who mend strained family relationships with pancakes made from a mix. But these stories aren't really stories, just false promises.

AN EXPANDED SENSE OF SELF

The concept of self that identifies us with our physical bodies, and/or with our possessions, is a very limited one. An expanded vision of self is one that acknowledges the world of our concerns, and the central relationships in our lives, as essential parts of who we are.

In embracing an identity that is larger than the boundaries of the physical self and the objects or resources that one owns or controls, it becomes possible to escape the trap of consumerism. For example, if a concern about the environment becomes a part of who you are, then choosing the organic milk becomes a way of affirming a connection to the rest of the world and making real this larger sense of self. When you embrace a larger sense of self, then it becomes a central task to heal and repair the world of your concerns and make it flourish.

The foremost task, then, if we are to escape the emptiness that fuels eating disorders, is to reweave a web of connectedness. Each stage in our technological and economic development has distanced us further from the rest of creation. Marshall McLuhan's famous dictum that every new technology is an amputation is nowhere more apt than in our relationship with food, and through food with the rest of creation. We have gained tremendously in mastery, but at the same time we have lost connection. The skill of bread-making is an elaboration of the self that is lost when we rely exclusively on store-bought bread, just as a dimension of the self is lost when we play recorded music instead of making it ourselves.

In an era when most people lived on the land and grew most of their own food, and when families and communities depended on one another in very direct ways to put bread on their tables, the sense of connectedness to the rest of creation was more immediate. The animals that were eaten were animals with whom the farmer shared a life and an interdependence. Since then, there have been a succession of distancing steps: from the marketplace, where the chicken was sold live; to the butcher shop, where the chicken was sold killed and dressed; to the supermarket, where the chicken is sold on a Styrofoam tray covered in plastic or has been transformed into something totally unrecognizable: breaded nuggets, a frozen entrée, or boneless marinated strips in a box with a picture of a former Miss America on the cover.

To create an alternate identity, we are going to have to create an alternate reality. It's not quite as paradoxical as it sounds, since we already have, in the cluttered closets of our personalities, most of the stuff we need: ideals, dreams, desires, and, in our cultural memory, enough of a shared vision of what this other reality could look like. We may not agree on all the details, but once we start talking about it, it's amazing how quickly those visions of a better world can spring back to life.

Idealism is not particularly fashionable today, for a variety of reasons. For some the problem is "compassion fatigue," a loss of hope in the possibility of change. For others it is a pervasive skepticism about the very possibility of altruism: the thought that every idealistic act must be either self-serving or self-deluded. But ideals really entail having a vision of the self within a larger frame. To live a bigger life, it is necessary to weave it on a larger loom.

A bigger life is one in which our story is interwoven in long strands with the life stories of others, in a fabric that stretches over lifetimes, that gives our most intimate relationships the "bonds more durable than love itself can forge." For the narratives of our lives to make sense, they must be stories that are shared, whose meaning is confirmed by others.

FOOD AND THE HUNGER FOR MEANING

Food has since time immemorial been at the center of the ceremonies whereby people celebrate their connections to one another. And this is what the inner emptiness that fuels consumerism and our compulsive eating is all about: a hunger for connection. It is connection that gives meaning to our lives, in the most literal sense of the term. The vocabulary that we have for understanding and expressing who we are is something that we acquire through being part of a language community, and our sense of who we are is created and sustained through participation in such a community. The more coherent the community, the more coherent and meaningful our lives can be; the more fragmented and incoherent it becomes, the more fragmented our individual senses of self become as well.

Today we face a crisis in meaning that is not unlike the environmental crisis that threatens our soil, water, and air. Just as new technologies for the production of consumables threaten to overwhelm the capacities of the earth's physical resources, new information technologies are testing the limits of the capacity of language to carry meaning. The information explosion has turned information into a form of industrial waste. It has acquired a status not unlike that of the Reichsmark after World War I: It is available by the wheelbarrow, but a wheelbarrow load will hardly buy a loaf of bread. One cause for the devaluation is that the information is increasingly disconnected from action: As with the commodities that clutter the consumer lifestyle, we have far more information than we need, but little idea of what to do with it and no place to put it.

Language as a tool originally evolved in the context of small local communities. The information conveyed by language has always been a little like money, in that its value was backed by the full faith and credibility of the issuer. Its original purpose was closely connected to action. Its usefulness as a tool was dependent on the coherence of its meanings. And language in face-to-face contexts never conveys only information. It always establishes a connection between speaker and listener.

Today face-to-face communication has been overwhelmed by mass communication, and mass communication has been transformed almost entirely into a tool for the marketing of consumables. Thus, we are constantly exposed to uses of language that exploit meaning in the service of selling. The traditional meanings of words and symbols are systematically exploited, and distorted, in order to create new connections in our minds: between buying fast-food tacos from a particular chain and being attractive to members of the opposite sex; between buying a brand of cereal and being hip. This is the sea in which our words swim, and as it becomes polluted, the understandings that we convey when we talk to one another or when we try to understand ourselves cannot avoid being damaged.

We can then imagine an analogy to the other kind of hunger. Just as it is easy to imagine that our food cravings may in part be rooted in the absence of some vital but undetected nutrients that are lost in food processing, we can imagine that there is something we call meaning (though we aren't sure what it is), that is lost when we consume too much of a processed-information diet. Just as health experts today recommend washing commercially grown vegetables to remove any residues of toxic agricultural chemicals, we need to wash off the meanings attached by the consumer culture to our commercially marketed food.

One very important way of meeting our daily dietary need for direct communication and participation in community is the sharing of food. Another practical way of reappropriating the meaning of food is to precede each meal with a ritual in which you assert that the food you are about to eat has some meaning in your life other than what is asserted by the packaging. For some people the traditional religious formulations may be an appropriate way to do this, while others may want to develop new language that better captures what food means to them. You don't have to believe in the guy with the long white beard in order to say grace. Saying grace can also be a summoning of yourself to mindfulness, and a more focused appreciation of the goodness of eating, living, and sharing food.

EATING MINDFULLY

It is one of the symptoms of our fragmented times, and fragmented lives, that we spend much of our time trying to do to several things at once—eating while reading the newspaper, talking on the phone while watching television, going through the motions of work while fantasizing about being somewhere else, doing something else.

Much compulsive eating is mindless in this way. The chips and guacamole sit in front of us, and so we eat them until they are gone, but if you asked us how they tasted, we might hardly be able to tell you. The eating was really a sort of gobbling, driven by an inner emptiness, or else merely by habit.

Mindfulness consists in being aware of and fully experiencing the present moment. Mindlessness is such a constant habit that it takes a real effort, over and over again, to summon oneself back from a flight of fancy and really taste the peach. At the risk of reducing the ancient wisdom of the Orient to just another weight-loss gimmick, it should be noted that when you eat mindfully, pausing to take note of the flavor and the texture of the food, and of the sensations on the tongue, you're likely to eat more slowly, and to eat less.

Because eating mindfully intensifies the experience of eating, we can often be content with simpler foods; a simple tangerine, eaten deliberately, one section at a time, can be a richer sensory experience than a big slice of Black Forest torte, eaten distractedly. But this same conscious eating may also make us more exacting about what we eat: The difference between flavorless, cottony white bread and whole-grain bread becomes dramatic.

And eating mindfully means eating with an ever-increasing awareness of our connectedness to the food we eat. The story behind the food becomes more interesting to us because it becomes part of the experience of eating. If you have ever eaten a tomato that you grew yourself, you know that. It really does taste better than the hard, gas-ripened tomatoes you can buy at the supermarket. But it may also taste better than even the tomatoes you can buy in season at the farmers' market, simply *because* you know that you grew it yourself.

EATING ETHICALLY

If food is the symptom of a larger problem—a hunger for meaning in our lives—perhaps it can also be the key to a solution. We can make choices about the role we want food to play in our lives that reflect who we are, what we value, and the kinds of persons we want to be. Putting these choices into practice doesn't just give shape to our diet; it also gives shape to our sense of self. We become persons whose most basic daily choices are guided by principles.

But what principles? Amid the moral chaos we live in, it is hard to know what to make of the various arguments we hear about animal rights, animal welfare, environmental destruction, and the just treatment of the workers who labor to produce our food. Do animals have rights? Is it immoral to eat beef from cattle raised on grazing land that was once rainforest?

Traditionally it has been customary to try to answer these moral questions in essentially legal terms. Sophisticated arguments have been developed to establish that animals cannot have rights, and that therefore it cannot be wrong to kill or eat them. That legalistic approach has traditionally been tied to the notion of an absolute source of moral authority. In earlier versions this was a divine power that could punish transgressors, either in this life or in the next. More recently this moral authority has somehow been rooted in the conscience, or in some notion of human integrity.

But as our faith in a divine power has crumbled, so has our faith in absolute moral authority. And with the rise of the therapeutic culture, the bad conscience is reconceived as something that can be made whole, not by penance and righteousness but by therapy, by learning to turn off those tapes.

The therapeutic culture's response to food guilt, as with any other type, is to run away from it, and there are certainly plenty of books and self-help gurus to teach us how to eliminate guilt from our lives. But their techniques rarely work, and when they do, the result is a sort of moral lobotomy, a loss of connection to our innermost selves. Thich Nhat Hanh cautions against the Western tendency to try to cut away those parts of the self that we find painful: "Therapists want to help us throw out what is unwanted and keep only what is wanted. But what is left may not be very much. If we try to throw away what we don't want, we may throw away most of ourselves."[2]

A better approach, argues Rabbi Harlan J. Wechsler, in *What's So Bad About Guilt?*, is to develop a discriminating conscience that recognizes when guilt is appropriate and when it is not. Rather than becoming slaves to guilt, we can listen to it, make peace with it, and try to understand its meaning. Some of its messages—like those that condemn us for not being slender enough or pure enough in what we eat—we can weigh and reject.[3]

But other messages from our conscience may have real meaning for us: Deep down, most of us really don't want to cause suffering to other sentient beings, don't want our standard of living to come at the expense of people we exploit, and do want to live in a way that is sustainable for future generations. And it's no surprise, nor is it wrong, to feel troubled when we feel one way and live another.

If we are not going to abandon morality entirely, we must find some other basis for holding on to it. To view morality as socially constructed, rather than handed down from the heavens, is not to diminish it. One of the paralyzing features of the postmodern condition is that all of our choices seem so arbitrary. Our most deeply cherished values are seen as merely the product of our time and place; had the circumstances of our birth been different, we might have a completely different set of values and tastes.

But it is only from the modernist point of view that this seems so problematic. All our knowledge and tastes may be located and inevitably parochial, but it is *our* knowledge; it is us. We may have to reinterpret the rituals of community, but we do not have to abandon them.

The connection between ethics and community is profound: shared values are what constitute a community. This does not mean that it is necessary to choose to be a part of a community that adheres to a rigidly defined set of principles (although those are often the most coherent and closest-knit communities.) Rather, it means that the work of developing and clarifying a set of shared values is part of the work of community building. But it is inevitably a part of developing a personal ethical code as well: A truly private morality is no more possible than a private language.

Moralities represent the cumulative wisdom of many generations, as they have struggled to solve the basic problems of how people can live together. That this is an ongoing and incomplete process is evidenced by the fact that these moralities still contain contradictions. The values of patriarchy and domination are deeply embedded in our culture, but so are the values of equality and connectedness. Reconciling those disparate values is our job.

We can only go so far through introspection, by asking ourselves which choices represent our most deeply cherished values, because often our own values contain the same contradictions as the culture as a whole. At some point, it is likely to be more productive to resolve these questions through dialogue. The conversation is of necessity an ongoing one; as the circumstances of our shared lives change, new problems emerge and new answers must be sought.

Thus ethical questions can never be answered entirely in the abstract. To choose one example, everything about the way meat is produced has changed, and so whatever conclusions may have been reached in the past, the issue must be revisited.

Arguably, for many of our ancestors eating meat was a necessity in a way in which it is not now. In traditional mixed agricultural systems, the killing of animals was part of a complex compact between humans and animals that gave something to each side. Humans sheltered animals from predators and augmented their diets, and in return exacted from them milk, eggs, wool, manure, and sometimes their labor. As farm animals approached the end of their productive lives and were no longer able to fulfill their end of the bargain, they were killed. Pigs were not required to work, but usually led much shorter lives than the other animals in the barnyard. Their work, in a sense, was to store food energy as fat and protein; in the winter, when plant foods were out of season, that energy could be consumed in the form of bacon, sausages, and lard.

To varying degrees farm animals were until recently still free to live "natural" lives (the fact that their 'natures' are the product of many generations of domestication and breeding notwithstanding): to run around the barnyard or graze in the pasture, to mate, to establish pecking orders, to nurture their young.

All that has changed in the last century, and particularly in the last few decades. Most animals raised for meat, eggs, or milk spend most of their lives indoors in confinement systems that give little opportunity for them to act out their social and biological natures. Because the animals are not biologically designed to thrive in these settings, a further series of interventions are necessary: Laying hens are mechanically debeaked, piglets have their tails cut off, and high doses of antibiotics are administered to control the spread of infectious diseases.

The environmental impact of livestock production has also changed as production has shifted from the family farm to the giant feedlot or pork operation. Whereas small-scale integrated farming systems recycled animal wastes, large-scale operations often create serious waste disposal problems. And, as meat consumption has risen, so has the strain on the earth's resources. Nearly all our meat comes from animals raised on feeds that require heavy inputs of fertilizers, herbicides, pesticides, and fossil fuels to produce. In poorer nations around the world, land that could be used to grow staple crops for local consumption is used instead to raise feed grains for livestock. In a global economy our own consumption patterns are part of the equation; some of the poorest countries of the world export beef to the United States.

It's a powerful act of self-affirmation to take these concerns seriously, to ask how your food choices can reflect your values. This can be a purely negative screening: You can choose not to eat veal, to buy only "free-range" chickens or "dolphin-safe" tuna, to eat no meat at all, to eat grapes or lettuce only if they are picked by unionized farm workers, to buy no food from tobacco company subsidiaries. But living your food values can also mean taking positive steps: choosing vegetarian and organic foods, shopping at food co-ops and farmers' markets, supporting food shelves and meal programs, becoming a partner in community-supported agriculture. All these acts are more than ways to avoid guilt; they are constructive moves toward creating a better world.

8

Planting a Garden, Changing the World

*What we eat is within our control, yet the act
ties us to the economic, political and ecological order
of our whole planet. Even an apparently small change—
consciously choosing a diet that is good for both our
bodies and for the earth—can lead to a series of changes
that transform our whole lives.*

—FRANCES MOORE LAPPÉ

Developing a consistent food ethic is a good starting point in the quest for a bigger life. But the real challenge is to put its values into practice.

CHOOSING A DIET

It begins, as Frances Moore Lappé has suggested, with consciously choosing a diet that is good for both our bodies and the earth. Such a diet, as it turns out, is also likely to be consistent with other ethical concerns.

But that is only a starting point. There are more fundamental ways of changing our relationship to food than changing our food choices. And there are also things we can do that may not necessarily seem to be related to food but that change its meaning in our lives.

Not everyone will come to the same conclusions about what ethical values to embrace, or about how to put them into practice. But some core values are very widely shared by people who have given serious thought to the ethics of eating: a desire to minimize animal suffering; a desire to ensure just treatment for the people who grow, harvest, and process our food; and a desire to use the earth in a sustainable way.

Our knowledge of food safety and nutrition continues to evolve, and—though it is likely that some of today's conventional wisdom about what is safe or harmful will be proved false by tomorrow's experts—there are nonetheless some major points on which today's experts seem to be in general agreement.

The preponderance of medical evidence suggests that the healthiest diets are those that are built around plant foods, with little or no consumption of animal products. Vegetarians have been shown to have significantly lower rates of heart disease, hypertension, constipation, obesity, lung cancer, coronary artery disease, type II diabetes, and gallstones. There is also some evidence that vegetarians have lower rates of breast cancer, diverticular disease of the colon, colonic cancer, calcium kidney stones, and osteoporosis.[1]

Research by Dr. Dean Ornish, of the Preventive Medicine Research Institute in Sausalito, California, author of the bestselling cookbook *Eat More, Weigh Less*, has demonstrated that a very-low-fat diet that is nearly or entirely vegetarian can greatly lower cholesterol levels and, when followed in combination with exercise and stress management, can actually reverse coronary artery damage.

Diets rich in meat and animal protein are almost inevitably high in fat and cholesterol. Toxic chemicals also tend to concentrate in animal fat, and so the higher up the food chain you eat, the greater the concentration of potentially toxic chemicals you ingest.

A plant-based diet is also good for the earth. Meat production has been described as "a protein factory in reverse." It takes far more land, water, fossil fuels, and agricultural chemicals to produce a pound of animal protein than a pound of plant protein. Eighty percent of the corn grown in the United States is fed to livestock. Much marginal land—the land most susceptible to soil erosion—that is currently used to grow animal feed could be taken out of production if the demand for meat were reduced.

This would not only minimize topsoil loss, runoff of agricultural chemicals, and consumption of fossil fuels, but it would also help restore some small portion of the biodiversity that we have lost and continue to lose. Most Americans have little awareness that the diversity and abundance of plant and animal life on the North American continent are but a small fraction of what the first European explorers found four centuries ago. We are living in the aftermath of a holocaust of the natural world, what naturalist Farley Mowat has called "a massive diminution of the entire body corporate of animate creation."[2]

Choosing a plant-based diet is also consistent with other widely held ethical concerns, the most obvious of which is with animal welfare. For some people the desire to minimize animal suffering may translate into a strictly vegetarian diet. Others may choose to draw the line elsewhere, to include eggs and dairy products, or to include fish and seafood, or even to include meat and poultry that is produced under humane conditions.

One approach that is gaining popularity is built around

the concept of "eco-kosher," a term first introduced by Rabbi Zalman Schachter-Shalomi. Following dietary laws can be one way of redefining the meaning of food; the idea of eco-kosher food seeks to reinterpret traditional religious values to make them applicable to contemporary environmental concerns. Thus Arthur Waskow, a leader of the Jewish renewal movement, can ask whether tomatoes grown by drenching the earth in pesticides are kosher.

His answer is that if the category of kosher is taken in its traditional sense, then it does not apply. But, he asks, "What if we both draw on the ancient meaning of kosher and go beyond it? What if by eco-kosher we mean a broader sense of good everyday practice that draws on the wellsprings of Jewish wisdom and tradition about the relationships between human beings and the earth?"[3]

The decision to follow a kosher or eco-kosher diet, or to say grace before meals, or to fast on certain days or during certain times of the year, all in some way engage and challenge the concept of food as merely fuel, and the earth as merely a tool for the production of food.

DIFFERENT CHOICES IN THE SUPERMARKET

To a degree it is possible to put these ethical values into practice simply by making different choices when you shop, without any other changes in lifestyle. Many meat eaters have already crossed veal off their shopping lists, and no longer order it in restaurants because of the exceptional cruelty of commercial veal production methods. To keep their meat tender and white, and to minimize feed costs, veal calves are kept in isolation in crates so small that they cannot turn around or groom themselves, and are fed a diet deficient in iron.

Another factory-farming practice that has been singled out as exceptionally cruel is commercial egg production;

laying hens in commercial operations spend their entire productive lives cooped in cages so small that they can't extend their wings, and are forced to stand on wire mesh floors that cut their feet. Free-range eggs, produced by hens that are allowed to nest and move about, are a good alternative to animal factory eggs, and can be found at farmers' markets, health food stores, food co-ops, and some supermarkets. Although free-range eggs typically cost 50 percent more than factory eggs, they are still a very expensive source of protein.

The alternative to consumerism is a relationship to food in which you don't simply buy food and eat it, but instead try to become part of a sustainable and interdependent food system. Trying to tread more lightly on the earth doesn't necessarily mean becoming a vegetarian, or buying organic produce, but it does mean using sustainability as a criterion in making decisions. For example, an organic head of lettuce hauled across the country by diesel-burning truck may not be any more earth- or community-friendly than a conventionally grown head of lettuce purchased from a local farmer.

All other things being equal, though, there is much to be said for organic produce. The evidence is inconclusive, but some research indicates that organic produce is nutritionally superior to conventionally produced produce—a superiority that might be expected since the chemical inputs don't replace trace elements that are depleted from the soil by conventional farming techniques. In subjective taste comparisons, organic produce and meats often come out on top. But beyond difference in the produce itself, there is a profound difference in the soil that produces organic produce. Organic soil is a living ecosystem, while conventionally farmed soils increasingly become sterile growing mediums, as dependent on external inputs as are hydroponic growing mediums. Organic farming practices put no hazardous chemicals into the environment, restore the complex biosystem of soils that have been damaged by chemical farming, and make far less use of nonrenewable resources. Moreover, organic farming has benefits that extend beyond the natural environment: Because organic farming is more labor-intensive, it contributes more to the vitality of rural economies and communities.

In a radically individualistic culture, we are encouraged to understand the issue of food safety in terms of the impact of what we eat on our own bodies. We are repeatedly assured that the use of pesticides is not dangerous, because when fruits and vegetables are rinsed, some of the pesticides are washed away.

But this leaves the question of wider consequences unanswered. Where do those pesticides go? It may be easy to wash them off our tomatoes, but is it as easy to wash them out of the water? Do they simply break down? Or do they contaminate groundwater or have damaging impacts on other elements of the ecosystem?

Eating Justly. Americans constitute 5 percent of the world's population, but consume 25 percent of the world's resources. If the whole world tried to consume at the level that Americans presently enjoy, the result would be environmental catastrophe. Our ability to consume at our present level is based on the premise of inequality: It is only possible as long as much of the rest of the world consumes far less than we do. (In fact, as emerging middle classes in developing countries acquire a taste for beef, the problems of hunger and environmental destruction are exacerbated.) The growing demand for meat results in both the diversion of farmland from producing crops for human consumption and the clearing of rainforests and other environmentally sensitive lands to increase grazing lands.

Paying a Fair Price. Another useful tool in trying to make your food choices reflect your values is the idea of a fair price. Try to imagine, when you look at the price of a bunch of bananas or a pound of beef, a second price tag, indicating what the product would cost if it were produced in a humane, just, and environmentally sustainable way. The difference in cost may be a saving for you, but usually someone or something pays the price. It takes 2,500 gallons of water to produce a pound of hamburger, and it has been estimated that without government water subsidies, ordinary hamburger would cost thirty-five dollars a pound. When nobody pays the true costs, the price is paid either in environmental destruction or in human suffering. We take for granted the vast desert landscapes of the American West; most Americans don't know that until large-scale cattle grazing was introduced, much of this region was covered by grasslands.

Sometimes the difference between the fair price and the price we pay is the result of the exploitation of someone or something. This is most obviously true in the case of foods imported from Third World countries, such as mangoes from Haiti and bananas from Central America. But it is often also true of produce grown in the United States and harvested by migrant workers. Many of these workers live below the poverty level and lack access to adequate health care, housing, and education.

Food isn't cheap—and when you pay little for it, that merely means that someone else is paying part of the bill. It could be a migrant farm worker family, who are paid too little to be able to live with dignity and hope, or it could be the land itself, which is being exploited.

Bananas—all of them grown in Third World countries and harvested by workers who earn only a few dollars a day—are the bestselling fruit in America. You may choose to eat bananas less often, or to look for organic bananas. In a widely publicized case a few years ago, more than two thousand Costa Rican banana workers became sterile after exposure to a pesticide banned in the United States. Organic bananas from the local food co-op cost up to three times as much as the nationally advertised brands, but perhaps that is what they should cost.

If you accept the idea that we have a debt, one response is to pay it back by contributing time or money to organized efforts to support farm workers and the environment. Another is to consume in such a way that as little as possible of your grocery bill is being paid for by someone or something else. The union label on domestic grapes, lettuce, and other produce means that the produce was harvested by farmworkers under a union contract that gives better wages, benefits, and working conditions than those received by most nonunion workers.

Most Americans find it hard to start the day without a cup of coffee, nearly all of which is imported. As Third World exports go, coffee is not as bad as some other crops; it is grown on hillsides that are often unsuitable for most other crops, and much of the coffee-producing land, at least in Central America, is owned by small farmers. But here too it is possible to make choices that reflect your values: Several American organizations have set up trading companies that ensure that the farmers cooperatives that grow and harvest the coffee receive a fair share of the profits.

Equal Exchange, a Massachussetts-based fair trade organization, imports coffee directly from democratically run farmers' cooperatives. This approach cuts out the middlemen and gives the small farmers a much larger share of the proceeds. For the farmers at one Mexican cooperative, working with Equal Exchange has doubled their annual income and made it possible to improve their health care, education, and transportation. The premium that Equal

Exchange pays for organic coffees is a strong incentive for coffee growers to farm sustainably.

Cheap food carries other hidden costs, which consumers and their communities pay. In the era of small neighborhood shops, the butcher, baker, and grocer were people you knew, and part of a richer social world as well. Today, most meat cutting is done by invisible immigrant labor at large packing plants, the meat is already wrapped and weighed when you find it in the meat case, and even the job of ringing up your purchase has been speeded up by automatic scanners. The self-service grocery eliminated the interaction between shopper and grocer. Supermarkets must be so large, and have so many checkout lanes, that you are unlikely to have the same cashier often enough to develop an acquaintance. You can't assign a cash value to those few words of conversation that you used to have with the butcher or the grocer, but you have still paid a price.

Eating Regionally and Seasonally. If you are trying to tread lightly on the earth, then one good way to start is by reducing your intake of foods that have been shipped thousands of miles. The energy costs of shipping foods—or in the extreme case, bottled water—halfway around the planet comes at a very high cost in nonrenewable resources.

Moreover, the quality of the food is often compromised in order to make it shippable—tomatoes, for example, are picked before they are ripe, and though ethylene gas gives them a red color, it does not truly ripen them. One helpful step in this context would be to rethink the idea of "natural" food. Why, for example, is a fresh tomato that has been genetically engineered to stand up to the rigors of shipping, picked green, shipped across country, and turned red with ethylene gas considered a more natural product than a canned tomato harvested at the peak of ripeness and processed in its own juices at a local cannery?

The flip side of the year-round availability of many fruits and vegetables is that they no longer seem as special. Scarcity once imposed a discipline on our lives as eaters that also gave it meaning. When oranges were so expensive that most Americans could only afford them as a rare holiday treat, they were a memorable experience, and one that we savored. When raspberries were only available for a week or two, those two weeks of midsummer were awaited with anticipation, and the berries were enjoyed as a special delicacy, soon to vanish again. Today anyone able to pay the price can have raspberries from Chile or California virtually year-round, but they aren't nearly the pleasure they once were. This probably isn't entirely a matter of perception; commercially grown varieties bred for yield, disease resistance, and sturdiness in shipping really aren't as flavorful as backyard berries.

They may also not be as safe. Regulation of pesticide use is not as strict in many Third World countries as it is in the United States. In their book *Circle of Poison*, David Weir and Mark Schapiro document the ways in which pesticides banned for use in the United States can still enter the American food supply as residues on imported foodstuffs.

SUPPORTING COMMUNITY THROUGH YOUR FOOD CHOICES

Locally owned food businesses, whether farms, restaurants, or food stores, tend to contribute much more to the economies of the communities they serve than agribusinesses and corporate-owned restaurants. They buy their supplies locally and keep money in circulation in the local economy. "If you choose to eat mass-produced, fast food you are supporting a network of supply and demand that is destroying local communities and traditional ways of life all over the world—a system that replaces self-sufficiency with dependence," says Alice Waters, founder and chef of Chez

Panisse, Berkeley, California. "And you are supporting a method of agriculture that is ecologically unsound—that depletes the soil and leaves harmful chemical residues in the food."[4]

The Food Co-op Alternative. Most American towns and cities have food co-ops and/or food-buying clubs that offer alternatives to supermarket shopping. Their philosophies vary, but most of them are committed to offering choices that reflect such values as social justice and concern for the environment. Co-ops often offer better selections and better prices for organic produce and bulk foods than do supermarkets or health food stores, and give end-of-the-year rebates to their members. At some, members who work a few hours a month are entitled to additional discounts. Co-ops are also more likely than their commercial counterparts to carry produce and food products from small, local farms or food businesses.

But the benefits of belonging to a food co-op go beyond price and selection. Even a few hours a week spent wrapping cheese, trimming produce, or working as a cashier can build community ties and create a better understanding of how the entire food distribution system works. Moreover, being an active member of a co-op offers a free education in the arts and challenges of democracy. Membership meetings are a rare opportunity to participate in democratic decision making.

Shopping at Farmers' Markets. When you shop at a supermarket, farmers receive only a few pennies for every food dollar you spend. Shopping at a farmers' market cuts out the middlemen, and keeps more of the money you spend in your community. Frequently the quality and freshness of the produce is also much higher. Truck farmers growing produce for the local market can choose varieties that may not ship well over long distances, harvest them at the peak of ripeness, and sell them the same day.

Community-supported Agriculture. The community-supported agriculture movement (CSA) offers urban consumers a chance to become partners with the farmers who produce their food. In return for a fee paid at the beginning of the year, subscribing households receive bags of fresh produce throughout the growing season. Some CSA farms also raise livestock. There is an element of risk involved, since a bad growing season can mean a poor return on your investment, but usually the arrangement is a good deal for both the farmer and the consumer.

Because the farmer receives a guaranteed income, many of the uncertainties and risks of truck farming are reduced or eliminated—an arrangement that makes it financially feasible for small farmers to stay on the land. The benefits to the farmer and the consumer are most obvious, but they extend to the larger community too. When small farmers stay on the land, the land stays in better shape than when it is converted to cash-crop (grain or soybean) production. Small farmers also support the rural economy and the rural social infrastructure. When their kids enroll in a rural school, they help keep the school's doors open.

The farmer has a guaranteed market for his or her crops, and the urban consumer gets high-quality produce, as well as the satisfaction of knowing that he or she is helping to ensure good stewardship of the land. And for those who want it, CSA farms typically offer subscribers opportunities to participate in planting, weeding, and harvesting, as well as special events such as potluck dinners and cider pressing.

Planting a Garden. If you don't have space for a garden, a window box will do. If you have never had a garden before, you may be surprised at how powerful an experience it can be to watch the seeds you planted a few weeks earlier turn into green, growing plants. And if you are open to such an experience, it can even inspire a certain reverence for the life force. It isn't quite the same as having children, but here too you have surrendered hostages to fortune: hoping that the squirrels leave the sunflowers alone and praying that the slugs find the little pans of flat beer you've set out for them before they find the heads of lettuce. This food will matter to you much more than any you buy in a store.

Starting a community garden raises it all to another level. It isn't only fruits and vegetables that take root when neighbors start a garden in a vacant lot; often it is the community itself.

"The pleasure of eating should be an extensive pleasure, not that of the mere gourmet," writes farmer and essayist Wendell Berry. "People who know the garden in which their vegetables have grown and know that the garden is healthy will remember the beauty of the growing plants, perhaps in the first dewy light of morning when gardens are at their best. Such a memory involves itself with food and is one of the pleasures of eating. The knowledge of the good health of the garden relieves and frees and comforts the eater."[5]

Cooking. There is enormous joy to be had in cooking—or at least there can be. In an age in which the surface predominates, cooking offers a different kind of mirror, particularly for those of us who have little opportunity to see the work we do to earn our livelihoods as a reflection of our creative capacities. As we transform raw materials into a finished dish, we see our own creative potential made manifest. And each time we prepare that dish, taking a few liberties here, adapting and adjusting there, adding new seasonings and new ingredients, we discover a little bit more of that potential. We realize our connectedness to the rest of creation by transforming it. The slow discipline of kneading dough, learning to achieve just the right consistency, doesn't just transform the bread, it also transforms us.

A homemade meal prepared for others has the same quality as a homemade gift; in this age of commodities the store-bought gift is just a more cumbersome version of the gift certificate, which is a slightly more decorous form of cash. The homemade gift, by contrast, is a gift of the self. Cooking as a shared activity creates a connection of a kind that is becoming increasingly scarce in the world we live in.

Americans are working harder than ever and have less time for one another than ever before. Given the busy lives that so many of us lead, it is hard to find time for this pleasure. But are we really too busy, or are we allowing ourselves to be fragmented needlessly? Making time to cook can be a way of taking control of your life.

RECAPTURING THE MEANING OF FOOD

Making conscious choices about how we consume is important, but ultimately it isn't sufficient. The kind of world we live in determines our realm of possibilities: To become the kinds of people we want to become, we have to create a different kind of world—or, as some might put it, to meet the challenge of our time, and heal and repair the broken world we live in. One important step in the process is to recognize and recapture the traditional social meanings of food.

Food now represents a whole vocabulary of possibilities. We can make food choices that represent our separateness, and our imaginary independence—for example, the single-portion microwavable fat-free frozen entrée—or we can make food choices that express our interdependence, and the necessity of maintaining a relationship of mutuality and nurturance with each other and with the earth.

Food has since time immemorial been at the center of the ceremonies whereby people have celebrated their connections to one another. Within the context of a strong spirit of community, even eating and its pleasures can be transformed. Whether it's at a church supper or a Sabbath dinner, at a block party or a family reunion, when we gather together to celebrate, when we linger in the moment, even the simplest fare can seem rich in our mouths—and our memories—without tasting the least bit sinful.

NEW SOLUTIONS

Given the hectic lives that many of us lead, it is hard enough to keep old friendships in good repair, let alone try to expand the web. But creative solutions to this challenge can be found. If you drop in at Dian Eversole's south Minneapolis house around suppertime on the second Sunday of every month, you're likely to find a crowd. Second Sunday, as it is called, has blossomed into a neighborhood institution. Neighbors tell their friends, and the word spreads. On some Sundays as many as sixty people show up over the course of the evening. To feed the crowd, Eversole makes a couple of hot soups and a salad or two. The rules are simple: You bring your own bottle, and you put your dirty dishes in the dishwasher before you leave.

When she started Second Sunday four years ago, not long after her son left for college, it was merely supposed to be a convenient way of keeping in touch with a large circle of friends. But it has evolved into much more than that. Eversole's very diverse collection of friends have gotten to know each other better, and the circle has widened. "There have been romances, jobs, and many new friendships," says Eversole, "people connecting and then going off and doing things separate from Second Sunday. People come here to check in and to know that they are wanted and needed. It really has created a sense of family."

Eversole makes enough soup and salad for fifty; whatever remains at the end of the evening can be eaten as leftovers the rest of the week. Occasionally it is the food that is memorable: a peanut soup, or a salad of potatoes, apples, and sausage. But more often it is the connections that are made.

Even the Internet can be a tool for building not only virtual communities in cyberspace but real communities in the real world. At least this has been the experience of the participants in the Pittsburgh Dinner Co-op, organized by graduate students at Carnegie-Mellon University. Members, who take turns hosting dinners, send out all their invitations, menus, and responses on the Internet.

In the beginning the motivation for starting the dinner co-op was practical, says Karen Zita Haigh, a graduate student—"to simply relieve people of the need to cook, without having to resort to restaurants." But over the years, Haigh writes, it has definitely developed into something more. "I would say that the primary purpose is still to eat good food but not have to cook it, but we do get a lot out of it from a social aspect. We are all from different parts of the world; about half are not American (including myself). This diversity brings lots of different viewpoints and ideas into the group, and we learn a lot about the world and about ourselves. Many former members keep in contact, and, a few people have even married other co-opers. . . . Eating, especially around people you know, is relaxing," Haigh points out. "Add in the fact that you are only responsible for the food once every three weeks, and it's very good way to reduce stress." And, Haigh adds, it's even a good way to learn how to cook. "Lots of people start out with simple things, and will get tips on how to make simple improvements. After a while, lots of 'simple improvements' become an amazing meal!"

The Pittsburgh Dinner Co-op has its own home page on the World Wide Web (Haigh is its designer), and another page listing people in other cities who have started dining co-ops, or want to start one. Nanette Longo, who lives on a small island in British Columbia, Canada, started a dinner club with two other couples in her community "as an opportunity to get together once a week for dinner without putting the sole burden on any one household.

"Three of the couples each have a young daughter, and we have chosen to include the girls. This eliminates the need [for] sitters, and the girls enjoy being included and the opportunity to visit with each other. Our format is quite simple. We rotate homes on a weekly basis. The hosts will provide the entrée (and set a theme if they so choose) and coffee, with each of the other couples being responsible for one of the following—an appetizer, a salad, or a dessert. Your contribution is decided at the previous week's dinner, so you have a week to prepare. We are all responsible for wine if desired, again to relieve the hosts of any great financial strain. Our club has given us a most enjoyable evening out each week (we chose Wednesdays to meet and stop the midweek blahs) and with very little expense."

BUILDING A BIGGER LOOM

The structure of the society that we live in shapes what we can become. When a community develops parks and playgrounds, it creates potentials for its children. When its citizens take the initiative to start Little League teams, the community builds on those structures to create even more potentials. Its children will not only develop physical skills that they cannot develop in a community without playgrounds but also relationships with others and ideas about their own identity and capabilities. As Harvard philosopher Robert Sandel has said, when politics work well, we can know a happiness together that we cannot know separately.[6]

Building community is a daunting challenge. Although it is easy to pay lip service to the ideal, it is important to be realistic about the degree to which community is possible or even desirable. A nostalgic longing for the Currier & Ives vision of community can get in the way; like Humpty Dumpty, that world has broken into many small pieces and can't be put back together again. Not only has our social world become fragmented, but so have we. We are now bearers of multiple identities, with loyalties to multiple communities. The friends and neighbors with whom we share some parts of those identities each have facets that we do not share.

ONE THING LEADS TO ANOTHER: FOOD AS A TOOL OF COMMUNITY

Participating in public life sounds a lot like eating spinach. Everybody knows that it's good for you, but hardly anybody really wants to do it. But that's at least partly because public life has become something like canned spinach: mushy and lifeless and with most of the vitamins cooked out of it. And just as Americans have in recent years discovered that spinach, properly prepared, can actually taste good, many are discovering that sharing food is a wonderful way of building community.

Too often the call for civic engagement has been framed in terms of altruism. We are called to act selflessly in order to help others less fortunate. But the call to rebuild public life starts from different premise: It is in our own interest to play a part in constructing a more vibrant civic world, and it is only when we are engaged in this activity as our project—and our passion—that we gain an enriched sense of who we are.

One thing leads to another. When the seven couples who live in the Kingsfield neighborhood of south Minneapolis started having monthly potluck suppers, their intention was purely social. But when they discovered, a few years ago, that the city had plans to widen the main boulevard that ran through their neighborhood, so that more of the traffic that runs from downtown Minneapolis to the southern suburbs could be routed that way, the issue naturally became a topic of dinner conversation. They worried that higher speeds on the boulevard would make the street more dangerous for children, and create a wall of traffic that would make it harder for pedestrians to patronize neighborhood businesses and parks. The potluck circle decided to work together to stop the project. By leafleting the neighborhood, they were able to attract four hundred community residents to a meeting with representatives of the city planning department, where they obtained a promise that the project would be abandoned. But the potluck gang didn't stop there. Several of the potluckers went on to organize the Minneapolis Livability Project. Their immodest goal is to turn their neighborhood into an urban village, in which a high proportion of residents can work, shop, and play within walking distance of their homes. Meetings of the project have brought together neighbors who had never spoken to each other before.

Where the institutions of community are strong, individual contributions to the common good can be rich sources of meaning in our lives: "I know him—he's the guy who organized our block club." "She's the one who got the new playground built." And that, ultimately, is what it really means to be somebody.

Notes

INTRODUCTION

1. Laurel Richardson, *The New Other Woman: Contemporary Single Women in Affairs with Married Men* (New York: The Free Press, 1985), pp. 88–92, as cited in Wechsler, *What's So Bad about Guilt?*, p. 21.

1. THE PARADOX OF PLENTY

1. Jacobson and Maxwell, *What Are We Feeding Our Kids?*, p. 7.
2. Meadow and Weiss, *Women's Conflicts about Eating and Sexuality,* p. 2.
3. *Glamour*, February 1984, cited in Bordo, *Unbearable Weight*, p. 334.
4. *Overcoming Overeating Newsletter*, February 1995, p. 3.
5. Jacobson and Maxwell, *What Are We Feeding Our Kids?,* p. 55.
6. Epstein and Thompson, *Feeding on Dreams,* p. xvii.
7. Jacobson and Maxwell, *What Are We Feeding Our Kids?*, p. 51.
8. Cited by Hillel Schwartz in *Never Satisfied*, p. 259.

2. THE FOODIE REVOLUTION

1. Warren J. Belasco, "The Two Taste Cultures," *Psychology Today*, December 1989, pp. 29–36.
2. David Steinman, *Diet for a Poisoned Planet* (New York: Harmony Books, 1990).
3. Jane and Michael Stern, *Square Meals* (New York: Knopf, 1984), p. 243.
4. Levenstein, *Paradox of Plenty*, p. 119.
5. Ibid., p. 117.

6. *You and Your Family's Food* (Washington, D.C.: Bureau of Human Nutrition and Home Economics, U.S. Department of Agriculture, 1950), p. 1.

7. MacKinlay Kantor, "I'll Take Midwestern Cooking," *Saturday Evening Post*, June 7, 1952, cited in Levenstein, *Paradox of Plenty*, p. 124. Of course, Kantor does manage to display his own familiarity with French cuisine.

8. Shapiro, *Perfection Salad*, p. 217.

9. Friedan, *The Feminine Mystique*, p. 11.

10. Bracken, *The I Hate to Cook Book*, p. 20.

11. Levenstein, *Paradox of Plenty*, p. 105.

12. Kappeler, *The Pornography of Representation*, p. 76.

13. Ehrenreich, *The Hearts of Men*, p. 51.

14. Kappeler, *The Pornography of Representation*, p. 76.

15. Peck, *The Baby Trap*, p. 14.

16. Ibid., pp. 15–16, 20–21.

17. Cited in Hess and Hess, *The Taste of America*, p. 174.

18. Beck, Bertholle, and Child, *Mastering the Art of French Cooking*, p. viii.

19. Hess and Hess, *The Taste of America*, p. 83.

20. Ehrenreich, *The Hearts of Men*, p. 45, quoting Douglas T. Miller and Marion Nowak, *The Fifties* (New York: Doubleday & Co. Inc. 1977), p. 119.

21. James Beard, *The New James Beard Cookbook* (New York: Alfred A. Knopf, 1981), p. ix.

22. Chalmers, *The Great American Food Almanac*, p. 9.

23. Lasch, *The Revolt of the Elites*, p. 29.

24. Shawn, *Aunt Dan and Lemon* (New York: Grove Press, 1985), pp. 95–96.

3. TRAPPED INSIDE THE MAGIC KINGDOM

1. Robert Wright, "Twentieth Century Blues," *Time*, August 28, 1995, p. 50.

2. John J. McGuire, "A Not So Novel Experience: Thrice-Fired Exec Puts His Accounts of Joblessness into Book Form," *StarTribune*, (Minneapolis–St. Paul), September 4, 1995. (The article originally appeared in the *St. Louis Dispatch*.)

3. Leah Richard, "Spirituality, Hope on Horizon as Solace Sought," *Advertising Age*, November 7, 1994, pp. 5–14.

4. *Advertising Age*, November 7, 1994.

5. Eleanor Early, *American Cookery*, quoted in Jane and Michael Stern, *Square Meals*, p. 243.

6. News release prepared by Fleischman-Hillard, a public relations firm, January 24, 1996.

7. William McKibben, *The End of Nature* (New York: Random House, 1989).

8. Aaker, *Building Strong Brands*, p. 172.

9. Guber and Berry, *Marketing to and Through Kids*, pp. 166–67.

10. Remarks at "Thirty Years Plus Five" restaurant conference, New Orleans, La., April 24, 1995.

11. Arthur Kroker and Michael A. Weinstein, "The Political Economy of Virtual Reality: Pan Capitalism," *C-Theory, an Internet Journal*, date to come, page to come.

4. WE ARE WHAT WE EAT

1. Sylvester Graham, *Lectures on the Science of Human Life* (London, 1854), cited in Griggs, *The Food Factor*, p. 58.

2. Shapiro, *Perfection Salad*, p. 6.

3. Christopher Lasch, *The Minimal Self: The Revolts of the Elites and the Betrayal of Democracy* (New York: W. W. Norton, 1995).

4. Gergen, *The Saturated Self*, pp. 6–7.

5. Cited by Veronique de Turenne, *Los Angeles Daily News*, reprinted in the *StarTribune* (Minneapolis–St.Paul), January 24, 1996.

6. Robert Wright, "Twentieth Century Blues," *Time*, August 28, 1995, pp. 50–58.

7. John McKnight, "Regenerating Community," *Kettering Review*, Fall 1989, pp. 40–50.

8. Miller, *Intimate Terrorism*, pp. 82–83.

9. Cushman, *Constructing the Self, Constructing America*, p. 207.

10. Ibid., p. 79.

11. Hirschmann and Munter, *When Women Stop Hating Their Bodies*, p. 135.

12. Twitchell, *Adcult USA*, p. 41.

13. Story and Faulkner, "The Prime Time Diet," p. 738.

14. Savan, *The Sponsored Life*, p. 5.

15. Bocock, *Consumption*, p. 68.

5. FOOD, SEX, AND THE NEW MORALITY

1. Burton, "Seven Sex Sins You Should Commit," pp. 34–36.

2. Carole Shaw, "From the Editor in Chief," *Big Beautiful Woman*, September 1991, p. 6.

3. Meadow and Weiss, *Women's Conflicts about Eating and Sexuality*, p. 6.

4. Baumgartner, *The Moral Order of a Suburb*, p. 12.

5. Ibid., pp. 134–35.

6. Margaret Thatcher quoted in Himmelfarb, *The Demoralization of Society*, p. 4.

7. Ibid., pp. 11, 12.

8. Jeffrey Stout, *Ethics After Babel: The Languages of Morals and Their Discontents* (Boston: Beacon Press, 1988).

9. Peele, *The Diseasing of America*.

10. Doherty, *Soul Searching*, p. 11.

11. Peele, *The Diseasing of America*.

12. Ehrenreich, *The Hearts of Men*, p. 45, quoting Miller and Nowak, *The Fifties*, p. 119.

6. THE GOSPEL ACCORDING TO WEIGHT WATCHERS

1. *Working Woman*, May 1994, p. 42.

2. Bordo, *Unbearable Weight*, pp. 199–201.

3. *Overcoming Overeating Newsletter*, National Center for Overcoming Overeating, vol. 2, no. 1, 1995.

4. Sandra Bartky, "Foucault, Femininity and the Modernization of Patriarchal Power," in *Feminism and Foucault*, Irene Diamond and Lee Quinby, eds. (Boston: Northeastern University Press, 1988), p. 81.

5. John Berger, *Ways of Seeing* (New York: Penguin, 1972), p. 47.

6. Frank Mort, "Boys' Own? Masculinity, Style and Popular Culture," in R. Chapman and J. Rutherford, eds., *Male Order* (London: Lawrence & Wishart, 1988, pp. 193–94, as cited in Bocock, *Consumption*, p. 102.

7. Bordo, *Unbearable Weight*, p. 201.

8. Susan Powter, *Stop the Insanity* (New York: Simon & Schuster, 1993), p. 9.

9. Ibid., pp. 12–13.

10. *Overcoming Overeating Newsletter*, National Center for Overcoming Overeating, vol 2, no. 1, February 1995, p. 2.

7. MAKING PEACE WITH FOOD

1. Raymond Williams, *Keywords: A Vocabulary of Culture and Society*, pp. 68–70, as cited in Ewen and Ewen, *Channels of Desire*, p. 51.

2. Hanh, *Peace Is Every Step*, p. 52.

3. Wechsler, *What's So Bad about Guilt?*, p. 14.

8. PLANTING A GARDEN, CHANGING A WORLD

1. Dixie Farley, "More People Trying Vegetarian Diets" in *FDA Consumer*, 1995, citing registered dietitian Johanna Dwyer, of Tufts University Medical School and the New England Medical Center Hospital, Boston.

2. Mowat, *Sea of Slaughter*, p. 13.

3. Arthur Waskow, *Down-to-Earth Judaism*, p. 117.

4. Alice Waters, "The Ethics of Eating," *Co-op Consumer News* (a publicaton of the Twin Cities Natural Food Co-ops), vol. 2, no. 1, July–August 1995, p. 4.

5. Wendell Berry, *What Are People For?* (Berkeley, Calif.: North Point Press, 1990), reprinted in Curtin and Heldke, *Cooking, Eating, Thinking*, pp. 374–80.

6. Michael Sandel, *Liberalism and the Limits of Justice* (New York: Cambridge Unversity Press, 1982), p. 183.

Bibliography

BOOKS

Aaker, David. *Building Strong Brands*. New York: Free Press, 1996.

Anderson, Walter Truett. *Reality Isn't What It Used to Be: Theatrical Politics, Ready-to-Wear Religion, Global Myths, Primitive Chic, and Other Wonders of the Post-Modern World*. San Francisco, Harper & Row, 1990.

Baumgartner, M. P. *The Moral Order of a Suburb*. New York: Oxford University Press, 1988.

Beck, Simone, Louisette Bertholle, and Julia Child. *Mastering the Art of French Cooking*. Vol. 1. New York: Alfred A. Knopf, 1961.

Belasco, Warren. *Appetite for Change: How the Counterculture Took On the Food Industry, 1966–1988*. New York: Pantheon, 1989.

Bellah, Robert N., et al. *The Good Society*. New York: Alfred A. Knopf, 1991.

Bocock, Robert. *Consumption*. London/New York: Routledge, 1993.

Bordo, Susan. *Unbearable Weight: Feminism, Western Culture, and the Body*. Berkeley: University of California Press, 1993.

Bracken, Peg. *The I Hate to Cook Book*. New York: Harcourt Brace, 1960.

Chalmers, Irena. *The Great American Food Almanac*. New York: Harper & Row, 1986.

Curtin, Deane W., and Lisa Heldke, eds. *Cooking, Eating, Thinking: Transformative Philosophies of Food*. Bloomington: Indiana University Press, 1992.

Cushman, Philip. *Constructing the Self, Constructing America: A Cultural Theory of Psychotherapy*. Reading, Mass.: Addison-Wesley Publishing Co., 1995.

Dewey, John. [1927] *The Public and Its Problems.* Athens: Ohio University Press, n.d.

Doherty, William J. *Soul Searching: Why Psychotherapy Must Promote Moral Responsibility.* New York: Basic Books, 1995.

Ehrenreich, Barbara. *The Hearts of Men: American Dreams and the Flight from Commitment.* Garden City, N.Y.: Anchor Press/ Doubleday, 1983.

Entman, Robert. *Democracy Without Citizens: Media and the Decay of American Politics.* New York: Oxford University Press, 1989.

Epstein, Diane, and Kathleen Thompson. *Feeding on Dreams: Why America's Diet Industry Doesn't Work—And What Will Work for You.* New York: Macmillan, 1994.

Ewen, Stuart, and Elizabeth Ewen. *Channels of Desire: Mass Images and the Shaping of American Consciousness.* New York: McGraw-Hill, 1982.

Fingarette, Herbert. *Heavy Drinking: The Myth of Alcoholism as a Disease.* Berkeley: University of California Press, 1988.

Foucault, Michel. *Power/Knowledge: Selected Interviews and Other Writings, 1972–1977.* New York: Pantheon Books, 1980.

Fox, Michael W. *Inhumane Society: The American Way of Exploiting Animals.* New York: St. Martin's Press, 1990.

Friedan, Betty. *The Feminine Mystique.* New York: Dell Publishing Co., 1963.

Gergen, Kenneth. *The Saturated Self: Dilemmas of Identity in Contemporary Life.* New York: Basic Books, 1991.

Griggs, Barbara. *The Food Factor: Why We Are What We Eat.* New York: Viking, 1986.

Guber, Selina S., and Jon Berry. *Marketing to and Through Kids.* New York: McGraw-Hill, 1993.

Habermas, Jürgen. *The Structural Transformation of the Public Sphere: An Inquiry into a Category of Bourgeois Society.* Thomas Burger, trans. Cambridge, Mass.: MIT Press, 1989.

Hanh, Thich Nhat. *Peace Is Every Step: The Path of Mindfulness in Everyday Life.* New York: Bantam Books, 1991.

Hausman, Patricia. *Jack Sprat's Legacy: The Science and Politics of Fat & Cholesterol.* New York: Richard Marek, 1981.

Hess, John L., and Karen Hess. *The Taste of America.* New York: Grossman Publishers, 1977.

Himmelfarb, Gertrude. *The Demoralization of Society: From Victo-*

rian Virtues to Modern Values. New York: Alfred A. Knopf, 1995.

Hirschmann, Jane R., and Carol H. Munter. *When Women Stop Hating Their Bodies.* New York: Fawcett Columbine, 1995.

Jacobson, Michael, and Bruce Maxwell. *What Are We Feeding Our Kids?,* New York: Workman Publishing, 1994.

Kappeler, Susanne. *The Pornography of Representation.* Minneapolis: University of Minnesota Press, 1986.

Kellner, Douglas. *Television and the Crisis of Democracy.* Boulder, Colo.: Westview Press, 1990.

Kline, Stephen. *Out of the Garden: Toys and Children's Culture in the Age of TV Marketing.* New York: Verso, 1993.

Kunstler, James Howard. *The Geography of Nowhere.* New York: Simon & Schuster, 1983.

Lappé, Frances Moore. *Diet for a Small Planet.* 10th anniversary ed. New York: Ballantine, 1982.

Lasch, Christopher. *The Revolt of the Elites / and the Betrayal of Democracy.* New York: W. W. Norton, 1995.

Levenstein, Harvey. *Paradox of Plenty: A Social History of Eating in America.* New York: Oxford University Press, 1993.

MacDonnell, Diane. *Theories of Discourse.* London: Basil Blackwell, 1986.

McIntyre, Alasdair. *After Virtue.* Notre Dame, Ind.: University of Notre Dame Press, 1981.

May, Elaine Tyler. *Homeward Bound: American Families in the Cold War Era.* New York: Basic Books, 1988.

Meadow, Rosalyn, and Lillie Weiss. *Women's Conflicts about Eating and Sexuality: The Relationship Between Eating and Sexuality.* New York: Haworth Press, 1992.

Meyrowitz, Joshua. *No Sense of Place: The Impact of Electronic Media on Social Behavior.* New York: Oxford University Press, 1985.

Miller, Michael Vincent. *Intimate Terrorism: The Deterioration of Erotic Life.* New York: W. W. Norton, 1995.

Mowat, Farley. *Sea of Slaughter.* Boston/New York: Atlantic Monthly Press, 1984.

Peck, Ellen. *The Baby Trap.* New York: Pinnacle Books, 1972.

Peele, Stanton. *The Diseasing of America: Addiction Treatment out of Control.* Lexington, Mass.: Lexington Books, 1990.

Postman, Neil. *Amusing Ourselves to Death.* New York: Penguin Books, 1986.

Rapping, Elaine. *The Looking Glass World of Nonfiction Television*. Boston: South End Press, 1987.

Robbins, John. *May All Be Fed: Diet for a New World*. New York: William Morrow, 1992.

Roth, Geneen. *When Food Is Love: Exploring the Relationship Between Eating and Intimacy*. New York: Dutton, 1991.

Sass, Louis A. *Madness and Modernity: Insanity in the Light of Modern Art, Literature, and Thought*. New York: Basic Books, 1992.

Savan, Leslie. *The Sponsored Life: Ads, TV, and American Culture*. Philadelphia: Temple University Press, 1994.

Schwartz, Hillel. *Never Satisfied: A Cultural History of Diets, Fantasies and Fats*. New York: Anchor Books/Doubleday, 1986.

Schwartz, Tony. *Media, The Second God*. New York: Random House, 1981.

Sennett, Richard. *The Fall of Public Man: On the Social Psychology of Capitalism*. New York: Vintage Books, 1978.

Shapiro, Laura. *Perfection Salad*. New York: Farrar, Straus & Giroux, 1986.

Thompson, William Irwin. *The American Replacement of Nature: The Everyday Acts and Outrageous Evolution of Economic Life*. New York: Doubleday Currency, 1991.

Twitchell, James. *Adcult USA*. New York: Columbia University Press, 1995.

Waskow, Arthur. *Down-to-Earth Judaism: Food, Money, Sex, and the Rest of Life*. New York: William Morrow, 1995.

Wechsler, Harlan J. *What's So Bad About Guilt?: Learning to Live with It Since We Can't Live without It*. New York: Simon & Schuster, 1990.

ARTICLES

Burton, Isabel. "Seven Sex Sins You Should Commit." *Marie Claire,* February 1996, pp. 34–36.

Story, Mary, and Patricia Faulkner. "The Prime Time Diet: A Content Analysis of Eating Behavior and Food Messages in Television Program Content and Commercials." *American Journal of Public Health,* vol. 80, no. 6 (June 1990).

Index